Praise for
HOW TO CREATE YOUR OWN
AFRICAN AMERICAN LIBRARY

"Like a farmer sowing seed, Dorothy Ferebee's carefully chosen selections for an African American library supply both essential guidance for newcomers to a literature more discussed than read, and the groundwork for delicious debate among avid readers of this genre over the author's choices."

—DERRICK BELL, author of *Ethical Ambition:*
Living a Life of Meaning and Worth
and *Faces at the Bottom of the Well:*
The Permanence of Racism

"Dorothy Ferebee has done the hard work of amassing and categorizing an impressive body of African American works, historical and contemporary, fiction and nonfiction, and made them easy to navigate for the reader and collector. Thank goodness someone's organized this at last."

—LALITA TADEMY, author of *Cane River*

HOW TO CREATE YOUR OWN
AFRICAN AMERICAN LIBRARY

DOROTHY L. FEREBEE

BALLANTINE BOOKS · NEW YORK

Ibae baen tonu...

Bertha Wyche Ferebee Chase
August 4, 1920 ~ August 20, 1970
Mom, thanks for all the books...

Olúre Hassan Perry
April 3, 2001 ~ June 5, 2001
Big Dad, you did your best...

Oba Omi Toki Alfred Davis
December 15, 1930 ~ August 19, 2002
Thanks for all the love, Baba...

Modupe Gbogbo Egun

———————

Maferefun Olofi
Maferefun Oshun
Maferefun Aganju
Maferefun Yemaya
Maferefun Orunmila

Modupe Gbogbo Orisha

ACKNOWLEDGMENTS

My eternal gratitude and love to Jillian Manus, agent extraordinaire, for making my dream come true. To Anita Diggs, for the opportunity to do what I love. To my editor, Elisabeth Dyssegaard, for being a joyous spirit and treating this book like it was her own. To Natalie A. Marshall, for taking the time out of her already hectic schedule to compile and edit the children's books. You know your stuff, Baby-O. To the Imperial Kendra D. Wymes, whose advice, research and organizational skills with the index were a blessing. Thank you BabyCakes! To Julia Cheiffetz . . . for basically holding my hand through the editorial process. Thanks for the support and encouragement. To Roberta Shorrock, for proofreading and input—Berta, you really know how to use a red pen!

All my love to . . . My cousin, sister and friend Bertha W. Scott, from the beginning—thank you. To my best friend and fabulous daughter Kenesah, for being my sounding board and staunchest supporter. To my warrior son Akinloye P. Braheem—you were always on my mind. To my big brudah Ron Facundo Harris, for chasing the shadows away. To my kindred spirit Basherah Perry, for sweating right along with me. To my goddaughter and friend Jackie Brown—you truly are a blessing. To Jovan Adé Perry—now I can come out to play again. To my Macomere, Lynette James—the heavens heard your prayers. Emory White, my muse—I'm back. Dewey Chester—then came you. To Joel Scott, thanks for standing guard. To Fred Brown . . . I finally did it. Now you can rest. Elsita Sotomayor—Mama, *yo te amo* . . . Lazaro Castillo Sanchez—*muchas gracias,* Baba. To Kaffie Sledge, for making me laugh when I wanted to cry. Terry Gross, for the many assurances that things would be all right. Danny Miller, for his friendship and for never once complaining. Amy Salit, for lovingly helping me build a magnificent library over the years. Naomi Person, for encouraging me to follow my bliss. Phyllis Myers, for years of keeping me on my toes. Ellen Morano, MS Word Maven, a whole heap of thanks . . .

To all my family and friends . . . thanks for understanding and supporting me during my time of madness.

CONTENTS

CONTENTS

INTRODUCTION

When I was about eleven years old I began to hate books and did everything in my power to avoid reading. My mother was self-employed as a dressmaker, milliner and baker. In the evenings she read magazines such as *Vogue, Redbook, House and Garden* and *Ladies' Home Journal.* They fueled her creativity. There was always a Book of the Month novel in the bookrack next to her favorite chair. She liked to collect antiques, grow roses and re-upholster antique furniture. Because she read magazines like *House Beautiful* and *Home and Garden,* my mother was able to create a home environment that belied the fact that we were as poor as church mice. Life was good.

My dad worked hard in the meat-cutting industry, the steel in-dustry, and as a roofer. When he came home, he liked a cold beer and the *Philadelphia Daily News.* He also seemed to "consume" pocket novels at an unbelievable rate. His genre was mystery and I saw a lot of Mickey Spillane, Erle Stanley Gardner, Raymond Chandler, and Dashiell Hammett. He had never gone beyond eighth grade, but we used to call him "the human encyclopedia." I never knew how he gathered so much information.

I didn't think there was anything particularly odd about my parents' choice of reading material, not until my mother started buying books for me to read right after elementary school. I didn't see any reason why I couldn't read her magazines and Dad's pocketbooks. I almost got caught with my dad's copy of *Lady Chatterley's Lover.* I knew it was forbidden territory because it was upstairs in his night-table drawer, and not in plain sight. I read chapters of it anyway.

My mother's book selections for me stunk. When you're eleven years old *Pilgrim's Progress* and *The Odyssey* are really not fun books to keep you company indoors while all the neighborhood kids are out playing half-ball and jump rope. *Lady Chatterley's Lover* at least had some information that I could share with my romantically unenlightened buddies.

Just when I thought things couldn't get any worse, Mom began to test me on the books I was supposed to be reading. I had to really read these books in order to see any daylight. Well, as the screw turns, all that changed when I figured out that she only read the beginning, the middle and the end. I realized I could get a good bit of the story using her system. I began to pass her tests with flying colors, but I still disliked reading. In time, I began to wonder what I was missing in between the beginning, the middle and the end. My dislike for books began to slowly fade as I got caught up here and there in an interesting chapter or paragraph. Now I was reading entire books and not minding them at all.

The first books I remember enjoying were *Heidi, Little Women, Jane Eyre, King Arthur and His Knights* and *Little Men.* By the time I reached junior high I was hooked on books. I was so addicted to reading that when I went to the bathroom, I would read the labels on the toothpaste, the mouthwash, the cleanser and the toilet paper wrappers.

It wasn't until I was in high school that I realized there wasn't very much in books that related to me, a young African American teenager. There weren't many black literary figures in my memory, except real-life people like Booker T. Washington, George Washington Carver, Sojourner Truth, Crispus Attucks and Harriet Tubman. I wondered, where were the stories about people who looked like me?

I began to have problems in English and History classes because there wasn't much there that spoke to me, or to my experience as a person of color. I became withdrawn and melancholic, which my teachers mistook for anger and belligerence. On my own, I read *I Know Why the Caged Bird Sings* by Maya Angelou and wept at the sad and beautiful emotions Angelou was able to evoke with words. The first book I read about a controversial black man was *The Autobiography of Malcolm X* by Alex Haley. It was thrilling to read an entire book about a person of color who was considered a hero by his people but feared by the government. Next was William Styron's *The Confessions of Nat Turner.* Why weren't we reading these books in class? I wondered. From that time on I made a point of searching out books about African Americans.

When I became a mother—to my daughter in 1972, my son in 1978—I looked around for books that would give my children a sense of identity and pride. Supplementing their steady diet of Richard Scarry's *Little Critters* were the few books written for children of color by people of color, like *Color Me Brown* and *Aesop's Fables.* I became a single parent in 1980 and returned to college. My goal was to get a degree in Literature, but I soon switched my major to Communications/Liberal Arts.

For the first time I was exposed to the writings of black authors like Toni Morrison, Alice Walker and Ralph Ellison in an educational setting. It was exhilarating and my bookshelves began to fill up rapidly with fiction and nonfiction by African American authors. I began to read books by black authors exclusively for my own education. Through these writers I began to see the world that shaped me and them. Here for the first time were people writing about the things I thought about and experienced.

In 1990 I joined the staff of National Public Radio's *Fresh Air with Terry Gross.* The show's emphasis on arts and culture opened a whole world of ideas and experiences through the guests who were interviewed. I realized it was important to be exposed to many viewpoints and areas of expertise. In 1998 I began to review books for the *Baltimore Sun*'s *Jubilee* magazine, which was geared to the African American family. I came to realize that restricting myself to reviewing only books by African American authors would exclude information that could be of enormous benefit. There is so much information out there that it is foolish to ignore what the rest of the world has to say. Many valuable books about the black experience have been written by people who are not African American or of color. So I created a website called BooksforBlacks.net to review books that are of value to the African American community.

How to Create Your Own African American Library is the outgrowth of my years of collecting books for my personal library and as a book reviewer for various African American mediums. I didn't grow up with a library in my home. There were bookcases, but there was no family library. The literature my parents read was for their leisure and recreation, not for growth and empowerment. The books they bought didn't validate my experiences as an African American child. But these books increased my curiosity and anxiety about my place in society. In fairness to my parents, let me say that they may not have been aware themselves that there was an abundance of great literature out there by African Americans and other people of color.

I decided to create a legacy library for my children and for anyone who needed and wanted to broaden their literary horizons. Over the years, children and adults have come to my house to borrow books, or to sit and look through them for papers and projects they've been assigned. My friends and neighbors know that my library contains books by people of color, not just African Americans, as well as by excellent mainstream writers who are not of color.

I believe *all* children should grow up in a home with a good basic library, especially African American children. Reading provides an opportunity to change places with people in other circumstances and cultures, to develop skills that are needed to communicate effectively in today's society. Books allow children to grow and expand their consciousness—to dare to dream. *How to Create Your Own African American Library* will get you started on building a strong legacy of literacy for your family.

African American men and women have been documenting their experiences since the eighteenth century. Through slave narratives, poetry, fiction, drama and music, their world has been immortalized with words. This body of literature is important to nourishing our collective spirit. These are the words of our community ancestors—words that still hold power and the ability to inspire generations to come. *How to Create Your Own African American Library* is my way of saying thanks to all the writers who have tried to leave the world in better shape than they found it.

Building strong people and strong communities starts at home. By building a basic library you put within reach the answers to many of your own and your children's questions, questions that might otherwise go unanswered. Oftentimes the questions are much more important than the answers.

How to Use This Book

How to Create Your Own African American Library makes it easy to start your own library. I've done the research and legwork for you already. The information listed on each book gives you five different options for finding your books:

1. **Name of book**—which also includes subtitle
2. **Author(s) of book**—primary author(s)
3. **Editor(s)**—includes authors of forewords, introductions and afterwords
4. **Publisher**—publishing house or series
5. **ISBN** (International Standard Book Number)—numbers that are unique to each publication

while also providing:

6. Number of pages—determines size of book
7. Most recent publication date—includes reprints, editions and reissues
8. List price, not discounted price

To get you started on *How to Create Your Own African American Library*, I've chosen subject areas that are the building blocks of a good African American library. These will provide valuable information and give you hours of reading pleasure. Through my research, I've unhappily discovered that many great books are too hard to get, or are simply out of print. Because of this I have had to leave out many categories and books. Still, the books I have chosen will definitely get your family library started. Just keep in mind: They are only the beginning of a great literary experience, not the end.

All of these books are in circulation in bookstores and on the web. If your bookstore doesn't have a book you want in stock, ask them to order it from the publisher. The web is an excellent resource for finding all the books listed. I have listed *paperback editions* for the majority of entries in order to avoid the more costly hardcover editions. You can also shop around for discounted prices. Each book is given a brief description—written by me or by the publisher. There is also an index in the back of the book to provide more information on authors, or subjects of biographies.

Before You Buy: A Few Things You Should Know

When I was sixteen I took an after-school job as a bookbinder, learning to bind and restore damaged books. This intensified my love and respect for books. In the late eighties I worked evenings and weekends with an antiquarian, Fran Emery. She taught me how to evaluate and appraise the old and rare books she bought and sold. Mrs. Emery taught me to see books as works of art that, if cared for properly, will last for many, many years.

It's important to know how to care for your books before you begin to create your library. Anything worth collecting is worth preserving and maintaining. I've learned the hard way not to drink tea near a book I am reading. And it's easy to set a book down to answer the phone only to have it crash to the floor and break the spine, which means your pages won't line up evenly anymore and your book will look crooked. The next time you think about sitting on your porch on a rainy day with a good book, remember that moisture is not your book's friend. Your pages will pucker and wrinkle in the most unimaginable ways. And never, ever, put a pencil, pen, or any other thick object in your book to mark your place. Always use a flat bookmark. Anything else will damage the spine of the book and cause pages to loosen from their bindings. The result is a book that closes out of alignment with uneven and crooked pages.

Spend some time learning about books. Become a bibliophile, someone who has a passion for books. Familiarize yourself with the language of book collecting. In order to have a library that will last from generation to generation, you should be familiar with the science of restoration and maintenance.

Keeping Your Books in Excellent Condition

1. Your shelves should be sturdy and straight. An investment in good bookcases now will save you money in the future. My preference for book storage is the Ikea "Billy" bookcase. It's inexpensive and very durable. If you have a bit more money to spend, you can invest in glass doors for your Ikea bookcases.

2. Books should be stored upright and not packed tightly on a shelf.

3. Books should not be stored in direct sunlight or in places where the temperature exceeds 70 degrees Fahrenheit. The humidity shouldn't exceed 50 percent.

4. Your books should be dusted every three or four months with a soft brush to prevent paper mites and dust from ruining the bindings and pages. Keep your books tightly closed when dusting the pages. Some experts suggest a soft, wide paintbrush for dusting.

5. Place your books at the front of the shelf and leave space behind for adequate air circulation.

6. Whole cloves placed in the corners of the shelf, behind the books, can prevent mildew.

7. Do not store books near kitchens or places where smoke and smells can settle in.

8. Check your books frequently for paper mites and other insects.

9. Put books back on shelves to prevent accidents that can damage them.
10. Make distinctions between books for lending and those you want to keep in good condition.

Making Sure Your Books Grow in Value

1. When possible buy first editions.
2. Author signatures increase value.
3. Do not write your name or personal information anywhere on the book.
4. Do not use bookplates on inner pages.
5. Keep book jackets in original condition. Repair tears on the underside with clear tape.
6. If you find fingerprints or grease stains on covers use a gummy eraser to remove them.
7. Invest in a good cleaning and repair kit, such as The Booklover's Repair Kit: First Aid for Home Libraries. This kit comes complete with an instruction manual by Estelle Willis, Wilton Wiggins and Douglas Lee and all the tools you need to make any kind of repair. You'll feel more confident about buying books of higher value as you create your library.
8. Remember, books are our friends. They offer us unlimited possibilities.

Nonfiction

*N*onfiction is real life. This form of writing offers one the most interesting, pleasurable and safest ways to trade places with other people, to experience a range of emotions—from laughter to sorrow—without leaving your chair. It is also a way to learn about something you may have always wondered about, but didn't have the time to explore yourself.

The books listed here are the ones I believe are the starting point for understanding the cultural origins of African Americans from before the transatlantic slave trade up till now. Some of these books are biographical, some are historical and some are personal journeys of discovery. Some of these books celebrate the spirit of the African American experience. All are vital in revealing the events that shaped the cultural identity of African Americans.

Some of these books will make you proud, some will make you sad, but they all will offer you a glimpse into a strong and beautiful culture that has survived all manner of obstacles and tragedies. These are books that you will want to share with your family and friends. These books will change the way you look at yourself, your family, your community and the society we live in today.

SLAVE NARRATIVES

The first writings in African American literature were narratives written by slaves and offer a firsthand look at America through the "peculiar institution" of slavery. These narratives were some of the first attacks on slavery that led to the abolitionist movement and the emancipation of slaves. They contain graphic depictions of life in bondage, including physical and emotional abuse, separation from family members and backbreaking labor from sunrise to sunset.

These stories provide a look at African American lives in slavery from every angle. There are narratives of household slaves, field slaves and slaves of mixed parentage. Their voices are filled with dignity and the quest for freedom and equal opportunities. While some of these books have duplicate narratives, I have chosen to include them because of other narratives they contain. These stories are the foundation of the African American literary tradition.

Slave Narratives
Andrews, William L., and Henry Louis Gates Jr., eds.
Library of America, 1,025 pgs., 2000, $40.00
ISBN 1883011760

Included in this volume: *Narrative of the Most Remarkable Particulars in the Life of James Albert Ukawsaw Gronniosaw; Interesting Narrative of the Life of Olaudah Equiano; The Confessions of Nat Turner; Narrative of the Life of Frederick Douglass; Narrative of William W. Brown; Narrative of the Life and Adventures of Henry Bibb; Narrative of Sojourner Truth;* Ellen and William Craft's *Running a Thousand Miles for Freedom;* Harriet Jacobs's *Incidents in the Life of a Slave Girl* and *Narrative of the Life of J. D. Green.*

Remembering Slavery: African Americans Talk About Their Personal Experiences of Slavery and Emancipation
Berlin, Ira, et al., eds.
W.W. Norton, 408 pgs., 1998, $49.95 with 2 companion CDs
ISBN 1565844254
The New Press, 352 pgs., 2000, Paperback, $16.95
ISBN 1565845870

Remembering Slavery is not a fictional account of life in bondage. These are real voices and real people telling their stories. In addition to the book, there is a companion audiocassette of the actual recorded interviews done by historians through the Federal Writers Project in the 1930s. The interviewers include Zora Neale Hurston and John Lomax.

Great Slave Narratives
Bontemps, Arna
Beacon Press, 331 pgs., 1971, $20.50
ISBN 0807054739

During much of the nineteenth century, slave narratives were best-sellers for American publishers. Arna Bontemps chose for this book three outstanding examples of the genre: *The Life of Olaudah Equiano, or Gustavus Vassa, the African, Written by*

Himself, the first of the slave narratives to gain wide attention; *The Fugitive Blacksmith*, by the first African American to write a history of his people in America; and *Running a Thousand Miles for Freedom*, an exciting story of a courageous slave couple's escape.

WILLIAM STYRON'S NAT TURNER: TEN BLACK WRITERS RESPOND
Clark, John Henrik, ed.
Greenwood Publishing, 130 pgs., 1987, $59.95
ISBN 0313259577

   William Styron's Nat Turner: Ten Black Writers Respond is a rebuttal to *The Confessions of Nat Turner* by William Styron. Styron's fictionalized autobiography of rebellion leader Nat Turner met with critical acclaim when it was released in 1968. The novel also met with fierce opposition from John Henrik Clark and other black writers, including Dr. Alvin F. Poussaint, Vincent Harding, John A. Williams and Charles V. Hamilton who accused Styron of racism and revisionism.

CLASSIC SLAVE NARRATIVES
Gates, Henry Louis, Jr., ed.
Signet Classic, 688 pgs., 2002, $6.95
ISBN 0451528247

   Henry Louis Gates Jr., chairman of Harvard University's Afro-American Studies department, brings four of the most recognized slave narratives together in one volume. *The Interesting Narrative of the Life of Olaudah Equiano, The History of Mary Prince, Narrative of the Life of Frederick Douglass* and Harriet Jacobs's *Incidents in the Life of a Slave Girl* all have two things in common: the triumph of the spirit over insurmountable odds and some of the earliest written accounts of life under slavery.

PIONEERS OF THE BLACK ATLANTIC: FIVE SLAVE NARRATIVES FROM THE ENLIGHTENMENT, 1772–1815
Gates, Henry Louis, Jr., and William L. Andrews, eds.
Basic Civitas Books, 352 pgs., 1998, $25.00

ISBN 1887178988

In the eighteenth century a small group of black men met the challenge of the Enlightenment by mastering the arts and sciences and writing themselves into history. The battle lines were clear: Literacy stood as the ultimate measure of humanity to the white arbiters of Western culture. If blacks could succeed in this sphere, they would prove that African and European humanity were inseparable. Without a literary record, blacks seemed predestined for slavery.

THE CONFESSIONS OF NAT TURNER
Styron, William
Vintage, 455 pgs., 1993, $14.00
ISBN 0679736638

In 1831 a slave preacher named Nat Turner led the only successful insurrection in the history of American slavery. Turner and his followers succeeded in killing at least sixty whites of Southampton County, Virginia, before he and his followers were captured, imprisoned and executed.

Turner's confessions to Thomas R. Gray, a southern physician, were the basis for Styron's fictionalized account. He won the Pulitzer Prize in 1967 for *The Confessions of Nat Turner*, but his triumph was short-lived when ten black writers responded negatively to his characterization of Nat Turner.

I WAS BORN A SLAVE, AN ANTHOLOGY OF CLASSIC SLAVE NARRATIVES
Taylor, Yuval
Vol. 1, 1770–1849: *Lawrence Hill Books, 832 pgs., 1999, $24.95*
ISBN 1556523319
Vol. 2, 1849–1866: *Lawrence Hill Books, 832 pgs., 1999, $24.95*
ISBN 1556523327

I Was Born a Slave collects the twenty most significant slave narratives and arranges them chronologically in two volumes to form a minilibrary of essential black writing.

VOICES FROM SLAVERY: 100 AUTHENTIC SLAVE NARRATIVES

Yetman, Norman R., ed.

Dover Publications, 448 pgs., 2000, $14.95

ISBN 0486409120

In candid, often blunt, narrative, elderly former slaves recall what it was like to wake before sunrise and work until dark; endure whippings, brandings and separation from one's spouse and children; suffer the horrors of slave auctions and countless other indignities; and finally witness the arrival of northern troops and experience the first days of ambiguous freedom.

AUTOBIOGRAPHY

Autobiographies offer the reader an opportunity to visit another person's life through his or her own words and thoughts, though sometimes with the aid of a professional writer. Some autobiographies are memoirs written at specific points in a person's life, while others tell an entire life story. Some authors are honest and forthright, but others embellish their lives or sanitize them. Autobiographies reflect how people see their lives, but most of all, they reflect how people want the world to see them. There are hundreds of autobiographies of African Americans. These are just a few of their stories.

I Know Why the Caged Bird Sings
Angelou, Maya
Bantam, 289 pgs., 1983, $5.99
ISBN 0553279378

I Know Why the Caged Bird Sings is the first of five autobiographical works that span seven decades. This is a story of struggle, loss of innocence and survival. It reads like fiction and one has to remember that it is Maya Angelou's coming-of-age story. When this book was first published, critics charged that the descriptions of child molestation and rape were too graphic, and felt that the book should be banned from schools. Angelou's honest telling of the story sheds a spotlight on how child molestation occurs and the effects it has on the child.

A Song Flung Up to Heaven
Angelou, Maya
Bantam, 289 pgs., 2003, $13.00
ISBN 0553382039

A Song Flung Up to Heaven opens as Maya Angelou returns to the United States from Africa to work with Malcolm X. But first she journeys to California to be reunited with her mother and brother. No sooner does she arrive than she learns that Malcolm X has been assassinated. Later, on a trip to New York, she meets Martin Luther King Jr., who asks her to become his coordinator in the North. King is assassinated, and Angelou completely withdraws from the world. Finally, James Baldwin insists that she accompany him to a dinner party, where the idea for writing *I Know Why the Caged Bird Sings* is born. *A Song Flung Up to Heaven* ends as Maya Angelou writes the first sentences of *I Know Why the Caged Bird Sings*.

Days of Grace: A Memoir
Ashe, Arthur, with Arnold Rampersad
Random House, 352 pgs., 1994, $6.99
ISBN 0345386817

In 1992, tennis great Arthur Ashe announced that he was stricken with AIDS. This book was finished only forty-eight hours before he died in 1993. Along with telling his life story, in his quiet, elegant way, Ashe points out the flaws in society's attitude toward people with AIDS. He recounts his days on the tennis circuit and closes with a letter of hope and promise to his daughter, Camera.

GO TELL IT ON THE MOUNTAIN
Baldwin, James
Laureleaf, 224 pgs., 1985, $6.99
ISBN 0440330076

Go Tell It on the Mountain, first published in 1953, when he was nearly thirty, is Baldwin's first major work. Baldwin chronicles a fourteen-year-old boy's discovery of, in the course of one day, the terms of his identity as the stepson of the minister of a storefront Pentecostal church in Harlem.

MANCHILD IN THE PROMISED LAND
Brown, Claude
Touchstone Books, 415 pgs., 1999, $13.00
ISBN 0684864185

Claude "Sonny" Brown's fictionalized autobiography begins with him lying on a dirty floor, shot in the stomach. From the age of six Brown lived for the streets, as did many first-generation blacks raised in the ghettos of northern cities. Brown was able to experience and transcend all the pitfalls that a young black male in Harlem could fall prey to and survived to attend Howard University and later law school.

A TIME OF TERROR: A SURVIVOR'S STORY
Cameron, James
Black Classic Press, 207 pgs., 1994, $14.95
ISBN 093312144X

How does a man face a lynch mob in 1930 and live to tell the story? James Cameron believes it was divine intervention that saved his life. The mob in Marion, Indiana, was throbbing with savage anticipation, calling for the deaths of three young men accused of robbery and murder. When Cameron tells his story, you are there with him throughout the beatings, maulings and abuses suffered at the hands of the mob. (See James H. Madison, *A Lynching in the Heartland*, in "Jim Crow, Segregation and Violence.")

GIFTED HANDS: THE BEN CARSON STORY
Carson, Ben, M.D.
Zondervan Publishing, 224 pgs., 1996, $5.99
ISBN 0310214696

In fifth grade he was at the bottom of his class. His classmates called him "dummy." He suffered from outbursts and temper tantrums. At fourteen, during one of his rages, Carson attempted to stab another child in the stomach. It was the turning point in young Carson's life. Today, Dr. Ben Carson is one of the most gifted surgeons in the world. In 1987, he successfully separated conjoined twins who shared parts of the same brain.

WITH OSSIE AND RUBY: IN THIS LIFE TOGETHER
Davis, Ossie, and Ruby Dee
Quill, 496 pgs., 2000, $14.00
ISBN 0688175821

One of the most celebrated African American couples share their story of falling in love, their courtship and marriage, raising a family and fighting on the front line of the struggle for racial equality. This isn't just a book about Hollywood and fame. It's a legacy from one heart told in two voices. Their story begins in the American Negro Theater, where they met. After half a century, they are still working together today.

TELL THEM WE ARE RISING: A MEMOIR OF FAITH IN EDUCATION
Hayre, Ruth Wright, and Alexis Moore
John Wiley & Sons, 224 pgs., 1999, $19.95
ISBN 0471327220

Ruth Wright Hayre grew up in a close, genteel family that had prized learning since the days of the Civil War. Hayre's faith in the power of education inspired her to take on her greatest challenge:

to create the "Tell Them We Are Rising" program. With that program she issued a challenge of her own to the sixth graders in two schools in Philadelphia's grittiest neighborhoods: graduate from high school, and she would pay their college tuition.

THE BIG SEA: AN AUTOBIOGRAPHY
Hughes, Langston
Hill and Wang, 335 pgs., 1993, $15.00
ISBN 0809015498

Hughes's autobiography recalls his conflicts with his racial identity, his father and his place in the world. Though he was heralded as a great poet and writer, Hughes chose a life that would not provide him with wealth and comfort. Very aware of the racism he would encounter from the white literary world, he was true to his desire to write about black life and black people.

DUST TRACKS ON A ROAD
Hurston, Zora Neale
HarperCollins, 320 pgs., 1996, $14.00
ISBN 0060921684

First published in 1942 at the peak of her popularity, this is Zora Neale Hurston's account of her rise from childhood poverty in the rural South to prominence among the leading artists and intellectuals of the Harlem Renaissance. By the fifties, her career as a writer had dwindled to the point that she had to accept menial positions in southern Florida.

THREE NEGRO CLASSICS: UP FROM SLAVERY, THE SOULS OF BLACK FOLK, THE AUTOBIOGRAPHY OF AN EX-COLORED MAN
Johnson, James W., ed.
Avon, 511 pgs., 1976, $6.99
ISBN 0380015811

Up from Slavery by Booker T. Washington is the autobiography of a man who was born a slave and went on to found Tuskegee Institute. *The Souls of Black Folks* by W.E.B. Du Bois is one of the first books of black consciousness. He was undoubtedly one of the first blacks to put forth the idea that there should be a cadre of black leaders who would guide the rest of the race. *The Autobiography of an Ex-colored Man* by James Weldon Johnson appeared anonymously in 1912.

SOLDIER: A POET'S STORY
Jordan, June
Basic Civitas Books, 256 pgs., 2001, $14.00
ISBN 0465036821

In this captivating memoir, June Jordan unfolds the day-by-day making of a poet and writer during the first twelve years of her life. Through Jordan's unfailing eye and uncanny ear the reader sees and hears how a great talent was forged inside a household both violent and loving, a childhood both idyllic and roiled by turmoil and conflict.

PASSING FOR BLACK: THE LIFE AND CAREERS OF MAE STREET KIDD
Kidd, Mae Street, edited by Wade Hall
University Press of Kentucky, 208 pgs., 1997, $16.00
ISBN 0813119960

In 1976, Kentucky state legislator Mae Street Kidd successfully sponsored a resolution ratifying the Thirteenth, Fourteenth and Fifteenth Amendments to the U.S. Constitution. Born in Millersburg, Kentucky, in 1904 to a black mother and a white father, Mae grew up to be a striking woman with fair skin and light hair. Sometimes accused of trying to pass for white in a segregated society, Mae felt that she was doing the opposite—choosing to assert her black identity.

THE AUTOBIOGRAPHY OF MARTIN LUTHER KING, JR.
King, Martin Luther, Jr., edited by Clayborne Carson
Warner Books, 416 pgs., 2000, $15.95
ISBN 0446676500

The estate of Dr. Martin Luther King Jr. selected Dr. Clayborne Carson to edit and publish Dr. King's papers. Drawing upon an unprecedented archive of King's own words, including unpublished letters and diaries, as well as video footage and recordings, Carson creates an unforgettable portrait of Dr. King using his own vivid, compassionate voice. Here is Martin Luther King Jr. as student, minister, husband, father and world leader.

A CHOICE OF WEAPONS
Parks, Gordon, Jr.
Minnesota Historical Press, 286 pgs., 1986, $14.95
ISBN 0873512022

Gordon Parks, photographer for *Life* magazine, writer, composer and filmmaker, was only sixteen when, in 1928, after his mother's death, he moved from Kansas to St. Paul, Minnesota. Parks struggled against poverty and racism. He taught himself photography with a secondhand camera, worked for black newspapers and began to document the poverty among African Americans on Chicago's South Side. This compelling autobiography, first published in 1966, tells how Parks managed to escape the poverty and bigotry all around him and launch his distinguished career.

ASSATA: AN AUTOBIOGRAPHY
Shakur, Assata
Lawrence Hill Books, 320 pgs., 1988, $14.95
ISBN 1556520743

When the pope visited Cuba in 1998, the U.S. government asked him to facilitate the extradition of a woman on the FBI's Most Wanted list. Convicted in 1977 in the shooting death of a highway patrol officer, Shakur was sentenced to life imprisonment. With the help of friends, she escaped from a New Jersey prison and fled to Cuba.

ONCE UPON A TIME WHEN WE WERE COLORED
Taulbert, Clifton L.
Penguin, 153 pgs., 1995, $12.00
ISBN 0140244778

Once Upon a Time When We Were Colored chronicles the author's coming-of-age in Glen Allan, Mississippi, in 1946. In a time when the Ku Klux Klan terrorized the streets and "Whites Only" were the first words learned by African American children, Clifton was encouraged by the love and kinship of a tightly knit community to overcome the bigotry and intolerance of the South, allowing him to embark on an extraordinary journey. *Once Upon a Time When We Were Colored* was adapted to film by director Tim Reid.

God, Dr. Buzzard and the Bolito Man: A Saltwater Geechee Talks About Life on Sapelo Island

Bailey, Cornelia Walker
Anchor Books, 334 pgs., 2001, $14.00
ISBN 0385493770

Cornelia Walker Bailey's family has lived on Sapelo Island, South Carolina, since 1803. Many inhabitants of the islands are direct descendants of Africans stolen from Sierra Leone, Guinea, Liberia and other parts of West Africa. Yet today their rich culture is endangered as young people move away for jobs in the larger cities. In *God, Dr. Buzzard and the Bolito Man*, Walker Bailey (with Christina Bledsoe) tells the story of growing up on Sapelo Island with humor and reverence for the ways of a people who made lives for themselves after slavery. From her birth to the present, her story is a fascinating journey of discovery and wonderment.

The Memphis Diary of Ida B. Wells

Wells, Ida B., edited by Miriam DeCosta-Willis
Beacon Press, 214 pgs., 1996, $14.00
ISBN 0807070653

When three of her friends, prominent black businessmen, were lynched by a mob in Memphis, Tennessee, Ida B. Wells became an outspoken advocate of antilynching legislation. Moving to New York after her life was threatened, she continued her tireless crusade against the "evils" of lynching. Her efforts to see antilynching laws passed took the form of scathing articles and essays in the black media. Her diary, in which she puts down thoughts she could never express in public, shows the woman behind the icon.

A MAN CALLED WHITE: THE AUTOBIOGRAPHY OF WALTER WHITE
White, Walter Francis
University of Georgia Press, 382 pgs., 1995, $17.95
ISBN 0820316989

Born with white skin, blue eyes, and blond hair, Walter White was at the forefront of the struggle for racial equality in the early years of the Civil Rights movement. As secretary of the Atlanta branch of the NAACP, White led a campaign to provide decent public facilities for African Americans. White was offered a full-time position at the national headquarters and assigned to investigate lynchings and race riots. Because of his light skin, he was able to gather information on the Ku Klux Klan and other separatist groups. (See his *Rope and Faggot: A Biography of Judge Lynch*, in "Jim Crow, Segregation and Violence.")

THE AUTOBIOGRAPHY OF MALCOLM X
X, Malcolm and Alex Haley
Ballantine Books, 496 pgs., 1987, $7.99
ISBN 0345350685

A charismatic speaker who practiced what he preached, Malcolm X rose through the ranks of leadership of the Nation of Islam. He held an illustrious position within the NOI until he began to see the flaws in Elijah Muhammad's organization. Once he made his pilgrimage to Mecca and separated himself from the NOI, Malcolm became a man marked for death.

BIOGRAPHY

Biographies are written about people who have touched the world both positively and negatively. Each story is unique and can affect people in different ways. Some stories may inspire people to strive for fame and fortune, while others may serve as role models and turn a person away from negative behaviors. There are hundreds of biographies about well-known and lesser-known African American musicians; literary figures; political, cultural and social leaders; entertainers and sports figures as well as people who've made the headlines. I've selected a few biographies just to get you started. With biographies, there's always something for everyone.

SLAVES IN THE FAMILY
Ball, Edward
Ballantine Books, 505 pgs., 1999, $16.95
ISBN 0345431057

Edward Ball confronts the legacy of his family's slave-owning past, uncovering the story of the people, both black and white, who lived and worked on the Balls' South Carolina plantations. It is an unprecedented family record that reveals how the painful legacy of slavery continues to endure in America's collective memory and experience.

WRAPPED IN RAINBOWS: THE LIFE OF ZORA NEALE HURSTON
Boyd, Valerie
Scribner, 528 pgs., 2003, $30.00
ISBN 0684842300

A woman of enormous talent, remarkable drive and rare intellectual prowess, Zora Neale Hurston published four novels, two books of folklore, an autobiography, many short stories and several articles and plays over a career that spanned more than thirty years. All of her books were out of print when she died in poverty in 1960, but today nearly every black woman writer of significance acknowledges Hurston as a literary foremother.

ROSA PARKS
Brinkley, Douglas
Viking Press, 176 pgs., 2000, $19.95
ISBN 0670891606

Rosa Parks admired King, Gandhi and Malcolm X but didn't rule out the "righteous use of force." The Rosa Parks who emerges from this biography is a true warrior, not some sweet, timid woman who accidentally stepped into a heroine's shoes.

ON HER OWN GROUND: THE LIFE AND TIMES OF MADAM C. J. WALKER
Bundles, A'Lelia
Scribner, 416 pgs., 2002, $15.00

ISBN 0743431723

Many historians and writers have researched and written about Madam C. J. Walker, but her great-great-granddaughter A'Lelia Bundles had access to records, photographs (some never seen before) and personal letters from her family's archives. *On Her Own Ground* is a story of how extraordinary things happen to ordinary people. Had it not been for her own problems with hair loss, Madam C. J. Walker might never have built her hair-product empire.

AN ORIGINAL MAN: THE LIFE AND TIMES OF ELIJAH MUHAMMAD
Clegg, Claude Andrew, III
St. Martin's Press, 400 pgs., 1998, $14.95
ISBN 0312181531

Elijah Muhammad, born Elijah Poole, dreamed of a better life than the one his slave ancestors had lived. However, by the time he arrived in Detroit in 1923, the bitter hatred and lynchings of the South had become a part of his consciousness, and the urban poverty and rank discrimination he encountered in the North further ignited his ire and indignation. In *An Original Man*, historian Claude Clegg reveals the motivations of this charismatic preacher whose life has been ignored for decades by both scholars and biographers.

IF YOU CAN'T BE FREE, BE A MYSTERY: IN SEARCH OF BILLIE HOLIDAY
Griffin, Farah
Ballantine Books, 256 pgs., 2002, $13.00
ISBN 0345449738

More than four decades after her death, Billie Holiday remains one of the most gifted artists of our time—and also one of the most elusive. Because of who she was and how she chose to live her life, Lady Day has been the subject of both intense adoration and wildly distorted legends. Now at last, Farah Griffin liberates Billie Holiday from the mythology that has obscured both her life and her art.

ROOTS: THE SAGA OF AN AMERICAN FAMILY
Haley, Alex
Dell Books, 729 pgs., 1980, $7.99
ISBN 0440174643

Roots spans seven generations beginning in the village of Juffure, near the coast of Gambia, West Africa. The first descendant of Omora and Binta Kunte, Kunta, would be the first of Haley's ancestors captured and brought as a slave to the New World. *Roots* became an instant classic because it was the first book to link present-day African Americans with their African past. In 1997, *Roots* was made into a television miniseries and watched by millions of Americans. It will always be remembered for the impact it had on American society.

KING OF THE CATS: THE LIFE AND TIMES OF ADAM CLAYTON POWELL, JR.
Haygood, Wil
Houghton Mifflin, 496 pgs., 1994, $14.95
ISBN 039570068X

Wil Haygood chronicles the rise and decline of Adam Clayton Powell Jr., Harlem's first black congressman—a handsome, flamboyant and charismatic firebrand. Haygood describes Powell's ascent to power from the pulpit of Abyssinian Baptist Church under the tutelage of his father, Adam Clayton Powell Sr.

Powell's fire was not restricted to the pulpit and politics. His love life reflected the same rebellion and fire that garnered him the love and respect of his congregants and constituents. Powell's political career was a roller-coaster ride of success and failures, and it was his success that contained the seeds of his downfall.

MARCUS GARVEY: LIFE AND LESSONS: A CENTENNIAL COMPANION TO THE MARCUS GARVEY AND UNIVERSAL NEGRO IMPROVEMENT ASSOCIATION PAPERS
Hill, Robert A., and Barbara Bair, eds.
University of California Press, 350 pgs., 1987, $21.95
ISBN 0520062655

Called "the most dangerous enemy of the Negro race in

America and in the world" by W.E.B. Du Bois, Marcus Garvey preached a message of black nationalism and separatism. He fueled the imaginations of thousands of African Americans in the Jim Crow era and led the largest mass movement in African American history.

RACE WOMAN: THE LIVES OF SHIRLEY GRAHAM DU BOIS
Horne, Gerald
New York University Press, 320 pgs., 2002, $19.00
ISBN 0814736483

Her husband was an icon, yet Graham Du Bois was herself a controversial figure. A champion of the Civil Rights movement in America, the liberation struggles in Africa and the socialist development of Maoist China, she was politically and culturally active long before she married W.E.B. Du Bois.

WOMAN OF COLOR, DAUGHTER OF PRIVILEGE: AMANDA AMERICA DICKSON, 1849–1893
Anderson, Leslie Kent
University of Georgia Press, 248 pgs., 1996, $16.95
ISBN 082031871X

When she died, Amanda America Dickson of Savannah, Georgia, reportedly was the richest African American woman in the South. Born into slavery, the daughter of Julia, a thirteen-year-old slave girl, and a plantation owner, David Dickson of Hancock County, Georgia, Amanda was legally a slave until emancipation. In 1885, David's will left Amanda, his only child, the bulk of his $600,000 estate.

W.E.B. DU BOIS: A READER
Lewis, David Levering
Owl Books, 816 pgs., 1995, $22.00
ISBN 0805032649

There is no historical figure more complex than W.E.B. Du Bois. David Levering Lewis sums up Du Bois in this way: "Always a controversial figure, he espoused racial and political beliefs of such variety and seeming contradiction as to bewilder and alienate as many Americans, black and white, as he inspired or converted." Drawn from thousands of essays, speeches, books and periodicals, *W.E.B. Du Bois: A Reader* reveals the essential Du Bois in a single volume.

This Little Light of Mine: The Life of Fannie Lou Hamer
Mills, Kay
Plume, 416 pgs., 1994, $16.00
ISBN 0452270529

Among the most important figures of the Civil Rights movement, Fannie Lou Hamer rose from difficult circumstances to dedicate her life to battling racism and poverty. Mills vividly re-creates the optimism and excitement of the movement, as well as the tension, uncertainty and danger faced by Hamer and her colleagues.

Sojourner Truth: A Life, a Symbol
Painter, Nell Irvin
W.W. Norton, 448 pgs., 1997, $15.95
ISBN 0393317080

Isabella was her birth name; Sojourner Truth was the name she chose for herself. The most recognized photograph of Sojourner Truth shows a tall, dark, imposing woman of pure African heritage. Though she was born into slavery and subjected to physical and sexual abuse by her owners, Sojourner Truth came to represent the power of individual strength and perseverance. Straight talking and unsentimental, she transformed herself from a domestic servant into a national symbol for strong black women.

The Life of Langston Hughes
Rampersad, Arnold
Vol. 1, 1902–1942: I, Too, Sing America: *Oxford University Press, 2nd ed., 528 pgs., 2002, $21.50*
ISBN 0195146425
Vol. 2, 1941–1967: I Dream a World, *Oxford University Press, 2nd ed., 576 pgs., 2002, $39.95*

ISBN 0195151615

This two-volume set is the definitive biography of Langston Hughes, the poet laureate of the Harlem Renaissance. Biographer Arnold Rampersad delves deeply into the context of Hughes's life. From his tumultuous relationship with his father to his travels to the South and abroad, to the largesse and patronage he received from admirers of his work, to his life as a Harlem literary intellectual.

DREAM MAKERS, DREAM BREAKERS: THE WORLD OF JUSTICE THURGOOD MARSHALL
Rowan, Carl T.
Welcome Rain, 475 pgs., 2003, $18.95
ISBN 1566492351

Carl Rowan draws on his forty-year friendship with Thurgood Marshall to write a biography that chronicles American history as well as the life of the first African American to sit on the U.S. Supreme Court. Rowan chronicles Marshall's reckless early years in Jim Crow Baltimore, his triumphs with the NAACP as the nation's most renowned civil rights lawyer—Marshall changed America by winning the landmark *Brown* v. *Board of Education* school segregation case in 1954—and his stormy twenty-four-year tenure as a U.S. Supreme Court justice.

ARTHUR ALFONSO SCHOMBURG: BLACK BIBLIOPHILE AND COLLECTOR: A BIOGRAPHY
Sinnette, Elinor Des Verney
Wayne State Press, 264 pgs., 1989, $19.95
ISBN 0814321577

This is the first full biography of the pioneering black collector whose detective work laid the foundation for the study of black history and culture. Born in Puerto Rico in 1874, Arthur Alfonso Schomburg came to New York after being militantly active in Caribbean revolutionary struggles. He searched out the hidden records of the black experience and built a collection of books, manuscripts and art that had few rivals. Today it forms the core of the New York Public Library's Schomburg Center for Research in Black Culture, one of the leading collections in the field.

NOTABLE BLACK AMERICAN WOMEN, BOOK III
Smith, Jessie Carney
Gale Group, 1,333 pgs., 3rd ed., 2002, $120.00
ISBN 0787664944

Narrative biographical essays, edited by noted scholar Jessie Carney Smith, discuss each woman's significant achievements and the public response to those achievements. Many entries contain personal statements from the subjects. This volume contains biographical sketches of five hundred women.

NOTABLE BLACK AMERICAN MEN
Smith, Jessie Carney
Gale Group, 1,000 pgs., 1998, $150.00
ISBN 0787607630

Notable Black American Men profiles five hundred contemporary and historic figures whose accomplishments will inspire students of every heritage. From the most prominent newsmakers to lesser-known names, this single volume features full biographical entries, four hundred photographs, addresses for living listees and recommended sources for further study.

CANE RIVER
Tademy, Lalita
Warner Books, 560 pgs., 2002, $13.95
ISBN 0446678457

Tademy takes historical fact and mingles it with fiction to weave a vivid and dramatic account of what life was like for the four remarkable women who came before her. *Cane River* is a story of four Creole women—Elisabeth, Suzette, Philomene and Emily. Each was driven by the desire to keep her family together and provide a better life for the next generation.

AFRICA TO THE NEW WORLD

The transformation from Africans to African Americans was made at the cost of many lives. Captive Africans leaped to their deaths in the waters of the Atlantic Ocean to avoid their unknown fates. Many starved themselves to death and many died from illnesses contracted aboard the ships. But along with their human cargo, the ships also carried the spirit of a people who were determined to survive.

The Africans had no idea what lay ahead for them. They were in an unfamiliar land, with strange people who spoke a language they could not understand. When they were first captured they worried if they were to be eaten by these strangers who held them in chains. By sheer will and determination, they survived and left a legacy of pride and endurance for their African American descendants.

BEFORE THE MAYFLOWER: A HISTORY OF BLACK AMERICA
Bennett, Lerone, Jr.
Penguin USA, 720 pgs., 1993, $18.00
ISBN 0140178228

Before the Mayflower traces black history from its origins in western Africa, through the transatlantic journey that ended in slavery, the Reconstruction period, the Jim Crow era and the Civil Rights upheavals of the 1960s and 1970s, culminating in an exploration of the complex realities of African American life in the 1990s.

MANY THOUSANDS GONE: THE FIRST TWO CENTURIES OF SLAVERY IN NORTH AMERICA
Berlin, Ira
Harvard University Press, 512 pgs., 2000, $16.95
ISBN 0674002113

Today, most Americans, black and white, identify slavery with cotton, the Deep South and the African American church. But at the beginning of the nineteenth century, after almost two hundred years of African American life in mainland North America, few slaves grew cotton, lived in the Deep South or embraced Christianity. Many Thousands Gone traces the evolution of black society from the first arrivals in the early seventeenth century through the Revolution.

SPIRIT DIVE: AN AFRICAN-AMERICAN'S JOURNEY TO UNCOVER A SUNKEN SLAVE SHIP'S PAST
Cottman, Michael
Three Rivers Press, 272 pgs., 2000, $14.00
ISBN 0609805525

When prizewinning journalist and avid scuba diver Michael Cottman participated in an underwater expedition to survey the sunken wreck of a slave ship off the coast of Florida, he was overwhelmed by powerful feelings of kinship and oneness with his African ancestors. In Spirit Dive, Cottman takes readers back three centuries and to three continents as he traces the complex and moving story of the slaves and the slavers. This is a powerful and compelling testament of one man's attempt to make sense of the history of his ancestors.

FROM SLAVERY TO FREEDOM: A HISTORY OF AFRICAN AMERICANS

Franklin, John Hope, and Alfred A. Moss Jr.
Alfred A. Knopf, 8th ed., 742 pgs., 2000, $49.95
ISBN 0375406719

From Slavery to Freedom describes the rise of slavery, the interaction of European and African cultures in the New World, and the emergence of a distinct culture and way of life among slaves and free blacks. The authors examine the role of blacks in the nation's wars, the rise of an articulate, restless free black community by the end of the eighteenth century and the growing resistance to slavery among an expanding segment of the black population.

THE DILIGENT: A JOURNEY THROUGH THE WORLDS OF THE SLAVE TRADE

Harms, Robert
Basic Books, 496 pgs., 2002, $17.50
ISBN 0465028721

In *The Diligent*, historian Robert Harms uses an entirely new approach to uncover the complex workings of the slave trade. Drawing upon the recently discovered private journal of First Lieutenant Robert Durand, Harms re-creates the macabre journey of a French slave ship and interweaves it with the remarkable dramas of its slave route. The result is an astonishingly detailed look at the voyage of a single slave ship that also sheds new light on the collaborative nature of the slave trade and how it shaped morality, politics and economics on three continents.

AFRICANS IN AMERICA: AMERICA'S JOURNEY THROUGH SLAVERY

Johnson, Charles, and Patricia Smith
Harvest Books, 512 pgs., 1999, $15.00

ISBN 0156008548

Africans in America: America's Journey Through Slavery, the acclaimed account of slavery in America that accompanies the PBS series of the same name, looks at the history of slavery in the United States, illuminating how Africans and Europeans built a nation. A riveting narrative history of America, from the 1607 landing in Jamestown to the brink of the Civil War, *Africans in America* tells the shared history of Africans and Europeans as seen through the lens of slavery.

SOUL BY SOUL: LIFE INSIDE THE ANTEBELLUM SLAVE MARKET
Johnson, Walter A.
Harvard University Press, 320 pgs., 2001, $16.95
ISBN 0674005392

Soul by Soul tells the story of slavery in antebellum America by moving away from the cotton plantations and into the slave market itself, the heart of the domestic slave trade. Taking us inside the New Orleans slave market, the largest in the nation, where 100,000 men, women and children were packaged, priced and sold, historian Walter Johnson transforms the statistics of this chilling trade into the human drama of traders, buyers and slaves, negotiating sales that would alter the life of each.

THE SLAVE TRADE: THE STORY OF THE ATLANTIC SLAVE TRADE: 1440–1870
Thomas, Hugh
Simon & Schuster, 912 pgs., 1999, $25.00
ISBN 0684835657

After many years of research, historian Hugh Thomas gives the complete history of the slave trade. Beginning with the first Portuguese slaving expeditions, he describes and analyzes the rise of one of the largest and most elaborate maritime and commercial ventures in history. Between 1492 and 1870, approximately eleven million black slaves were carried from Africa to the Americas to work on plantations, in mines or as servants in houses.

THEY CAME BEFORE COLUMBUS: THE AFRICAN PRESENCE IN ANCIENT AMERICA
Van Sertima, Ivan
Random House, 352 pgs., 2003, $14.95
ISBN 0394402456

Ivan Van Sertima offers a compelling argument on the presence and legacy of black Africans in ancient America, writing of an African presence in the New World centuries before Columbus arrived in 1492.

THE DESTRUCTION OF BLACK CIVILIZATION: GREAT ISSUES OF A RACE FROM 4500 B.C. TO 2000 A.D.
Williams, Chancellor
Third World Press, 388 pgs., 1992, $17.95
ISBN 0883780305

For sixteen years Chancellor Williams researched this classic of black history, spending two years visiting over twenty-six African nations throughout the African continent. What was to be a two-volume set of African history was synthesized into a smaller book due to the author's visual impairment. Often called the "bible" of black history, here is history that speaks directly to the experiences of black Americans.

RESISTANCE AND REBELLION

Depictions of slavery often include images of happy slaves singing while they labored in the fields and delighting in caring for their masters and their masters' children. Blacks were not resigned to their plight, as books and movies often portrayed them. They ran away with surprising regularity, oftentimes despite repeated beatings and maiming. Many slaves fled, using the Underground Railroad, a system of escape routes that took many slaves north to freedom.

There were also African Americans who resisted and planned to take their freedom by force. These slave rebellions were organized by charismatic leaders such as Gabriel Prosser, Denmark Vesey and Nat Turner, who believed they had nothing to lose and everything to gain. Many revolts were planned, although few were successful. Most of the time the rebellions were squashed before they were started because another slave would betray their plans to the master.

AMERICAN NEGRO SLAVE REVOLTS
Aptheker, Herbert
International Publishers, 5th ed., 428 pgs., 1993, $9.95
ISBN 0717806057

In 1943, Herbert Aptheker published *American Negro Slave Revolts*. Initially meeting resistance from established historians, this book is now considered the definitive work on the struggle for freedom from slavery. Aptheker was a close friend and colleague of W.E.B. Du Bois and served as custodian of the Du Bois papers, newspaper articles, journals, letters and other reports.

ALL SOULS' RISING
Bell, Madison Smartt
Penguin USA, 504 pgs., 1996, $15.00
ISBN 0140259473

Bell brings to life the slave rebellion of the 1790s that would bring an end to the brutal white rule in Haiti. At the epicenter of the rebellion is a second-generation African slave known as Toussaint L'Ouverture. Self-educated, favored and trusted by his master, quietly charismatic, bold in thought and subtle in action, Toussaint is determined to resist the excesses of the mob and still put an end to French dominion.

BLACK THUNDER: GABRIEL'S REVOLT, VIRGINIA 1800
Bontemps, Arna
Beacon Press, 254 pgs., 1992, $17.50
ISBN 0807063371

Originally published in 1936, *Black Thunder* is the story of Gabriel Prosser, a slave who decides to avenge the murder of a fellow slave by leading the blacks of Richmond against their masters.

Arna Bontemps's historical novel follows the rebel leader Gabriel from his beginnings as a blacksmith on the Prosser plantation to his rise as a leader of a Virginia slave rebellion, leading a thousand slaves armed with clubs, guns, bayonets and scythes to Richmond to fight for freedom. Prosser was betrayed by two slaves, Tom and Pharoh, who told their master of the plot. Gabriel still believed in the inevitable triumph of his struggle for freedom.

RUNAWAY SLAVES: REBELS ON THE PLANTATION
Franklin, John Hope, and Loren Schweninger
Oxford University Press, 480 pgs., 2000, $17.95
ISBN 0195084519

In *Runaway Slaves*, John Hope Franklin and Loren Schweninger demonstrate that significant numbers of slaves did in fact frequently rebel against their masters and struggle to attain their freedom. By surveying a wealth of documents, such as planters' records, petitions to county courts and state legislatures, and local newspapers, this book shows how slaves resisted; when, where and how they escaped; where they fled to; how long they remained in hiding and how they survived away from the plantation.

BLACK REBELLION: FIVE SLAVE REVOLTS
Higginson, Thomas Wentworth
DaCapo Press, 242 pgs., 1998, $15.00
ISBN 0306808676

In America there was Gabriel Prosser, who in 1800 recruited a thousand fellow slaves to launch a rebellion throughout Virginia; Denmark Vesey, an ex-slave, seaman and artisan, who conspired in 1822 to kill the whites in Charleston, South Carolina, and take over the city; and Nat Turner, who in 1831 organized and led the most successful and dramatic slave revolt in North America. The author also describes how whites responded with panic, sweeping arrests and laws in a futile effort to crush the slaves' insatiable desire to be free.

JOHN BROWN AND HIS MEN
Hinton, Richard J., edited by Carlos Martyn
Vol. 1, *Digital Scanning Inc., 424 pgs., $19.95*
ISBN 1582182949

Vol. 2, *Digital Scanning Inc., 356 pgs., 2001, $19.95*
ISBN 1582183562

This was the famous raid into Virginia by John Brown. A white New Englander by birth, Brown distinguished himself for his fearlessness and violence after the bloody struggle in Kansas where he hoped to strike a more effective blow for freedom. His crusade against slavery entailed a plan to seize the arsenal at Harper's Ferry, free the blacks in the region and retreat to a stronghold in the mountains. In the autumn of 1859 he seized the arsenal and began to free the slaves in the area. However, troops were quick to overpower the ragtag guerrilla group. Once captured, Brown and several others were speedily brought to trial, convicted and hanged.

BLACK MUTINY: THE REVOLT ON THE SCHOONER AMISTAD
Owens, William A.
Plume, 352 pgs., 1997, $12.95
ISBN 0452279356

Originally published in 1953, *Black Mutiny* remains one of the most detailed accounts of the *Amistad* revolt. In 1839, under the leadership of Cinque, the enslaved Mendi aboard the schooner *Amistad* killed the ship's captain and took control of the vessel in a valiant attempt to regain their freedom. Cinque's attempts to guide the ship back to Africa were thwarted by surviving members of the *Amistad*'s crew.

DENMARK VESEY: THE BURIED STORY OF AMERICA'S LARGEST SLAVE REBELLION AND THE MAN WHO LED IT
Robertson, David
Vintage, 224 pgs., 2000, $13.00
ISBN 0679762183

Denmark Vesey was a literate, professional and relatively well-off ex-slave who had purchased his own freedom with the winnings from a lottery. Inspired by the success of the revolutionary black republic of Haiti, he persuaded some nine thousand slaves to join him in a revolt. On a June evening in 1822, having gathered guns and daggers, they were to converge on Charleston,

South Carolina, take the city's arsenal, murder the populace, burn the city and escape by ship to Haiti or Africa. The uprising was betrayed and Vesey and seventy-seven of his followers were executed; the matter was hushed up by Charleston's elite for fear of further rebellion.

ABOLITION, THE CIVIL WAR AND RECONSTRUCTION

African Americans did not rely solely on the kindness and humanity of white people to end slavery. African Americans were also among the first antislavery activists and leaders. The abolition of slavery was brought about through the efforts of both blacks and whites. The Civil War was not just about the political and social differences between northerners and southerners and the state of the union, it was also about the eradication of the economic institution of slavery.

For a short time after the Civil War and emancipation, African Americans also participated in the reconstruction and governing of southern states. During the period of Reconstruction, which lasted from 1866 to 1876, African Americans were protected by legislation that made it illegal to discriminate against them. These laws were not accepted by southern whites and led to the Jim Crow era of segregation and violence against African Americans.

At the Hands of Persons Unknown: The Lynching of Black America
Dray, Philip
Modern Library, 544 pgs., 2003, $14.95
ISBN 0375754458

Men and women were shot, hanged, tortured and burned, often in sadistic "spectacle lynchings" involving thousands of witnesses. "At the hands of persons unknown" was the official verdict rendered on most of these atrocities.

Black Reconstruction in America, 1860–1880
Du Bois, W.E.B., with an introduction by David Levering Lewis
Free Press, 768 pgs., 1999, $19.95
ISBN 0684856573

David Levering Lewis introduces W.E.B. Du Bois's groundbreaking study of the aftermath of the Civil War, *Black Reconstruction*, which for the first time tied the cause of liberty for slaves directly to the Civil War. Du Bois put black enslavement at the center of America's war between the states. Through his writings, African Americans were represented in the history of Reconstruction.

Reconstruction: America's Unfinished Revolution, 1863–1877
Foner, Eric
Perennial, 736 pgs., 2002, $23.95
ISBN 0060937165

Reconstruction chronicles how Americans, black and white, responded to the unprecedented changes unleashed by the Civil War and the end of slavery. There are fresh insights on a host of other issues, including Abraham Lincoln's attitude toward Reconstruction, the conflict between Andrew Johnson and Congress, the extent of black voting and officeholding, the origins of "carpetbaggers" and "scalawags" and the role of violence in the period.

BEEN IN THE STORM SO LONG: THE AFTERMATH OF SLAVERY
Litwak, Leon F.
Vintage, 672 pgs., 1980, $15.96
ISBN 0394743989

Using previously unexamined sources—interviews with ex-slaves, diaries and accounts by former slaveholders—historian Leon Litwak shows how, during the Civil War and after emancipation, blacks and whites interacted in ways that dramatized not only their mutual dependency, but the ambiguities and tensions that had always been latent in "the peculiar institution." Litwak's sources were collected by the Federal Writers Project.

BATTLE CRY OF FREEDOM: THE CIVIL WAR ERA
McPherson, James M.
Ballantine Books, 904 pgs., 1989, $18.00
ISBN 0345359429

Battle Cry of Freedom is the best single-volume history of the American Civil War available. McPherson first describes the economic, social, political and technological changes that occurred in the United States in the years before the conflict. Then he describes the political environment in America that led to the election of Abraham Lincoln. This election precipitated the secession of seven and ultimately eleven southern states. The secession debate within the southern governments is explained fully. The war itself is described primarily in strategic terms, but with clear descriptions of the human costs of the conflict.

THE BLACK HEARTS OF MEN: RADICAL ABOLITIONISTS AND THE TRANSFORMATION OF RACE
Stauffer, John
Harvard University Press, 384 pgs., 2002, $29.95
ISBN 0674006453

At a time when slavery was spreading and the country was steeped in racism, two white men and two black men—Gerrit Smith, John Brown, Frederick Douglass, and James McCune Smith—overcame social barriers and mistrust to form a unique alliance that sought nothing less than the end of all evil. Drawing on the largest extant biracial correspondence in the Civil War era, historian John Stauffer braids together these men's struggles to reconcile ideals of justice with the reality of slavery and oppression.

HOLY WARRIORS: ABOLITIONISTS AND AMERICAN SLAVERY
Stewart, James Brewer
Hill and Wang, 256 pgs., 1997, $15.00
ISBN 080901596X

Fearful of secularism and materialism, and disdainful of the luxurious life of the upper class, evangelical Christians of varying ethnicities banded together to forge a religious revival called the Great Awakening. In the South these evangelicals, especially the Quakers, confronted slaveholding Anglicans. They steadily worked to convert pro-slavery individuals, and they were often successful. By recruiting escaped slaves to speak out publicly against "the peculiar institution," the abolitionists galvanized public opinion outside the South, leading to the sectionalism that would later find its ultimate expression in the Civil War.

FINAL FREEDOM: THE CIVIL WAR, THE ABOLITION OF SLAVERY, AND THE THIRTEENTH AMENDMENT
Vorenburg, Michael
Cambridge University Press, 324 pgs., 2001, $30.00
ISBN 0521652677

Final Freedom examines emancipation after the Emancipation Proclamation of 1863 and during the last years of the American Civil War. Focusing on the making and meaning of the Thirteenth Amendment, it looks at the struggle among legal thinkers, politicians and ordinary Americans in the North and the border states to find a way to abolish slavery that would overcome the inadequacies of the proclamation.

DAVID WALKER'S APPEAL TO THE COLOURED CITIZENS OF THE WORLD

Walker, David, edited by Sean Wilentz
Hill and Wang, 128 pgs., 1995, $9.00
ISBN 0809015811

In 1829, David Walker, a used-clothing salesman, wrote *David Walker's Appeal*, a small pamphlet subtitled *"To the COLOURED CITIZENS OF THE WORLD, but in particular, and very expressly, to those of THE UNITED STATES OF AMERICA."* It was called "the most notorious document in America." By using an underground distribution system, Walker put his pamphlet in the hands of thousands of plantation slaves. Southern whites put up a $3,000 reward for Walker's head, and offered $10,000 for him alive. Walker's friends begged him to run away to the safety of Canada, which he refused to do. David Walker was found dead in his Boston home in August 1830.

THE CIVIL WAR: AN ILLUSTRATED HISTORY

Ward, Geoffrey C.
Alfred A. Knopf, 448 pgs., 1992, $29.95
ISBN 0679742778

A wealth of documentary illustrations and a narrative alive with original and energetic scholarship combine to present both the grand sweep of events and the minutest of human details. *The Civil War* is not simply the story of great battles and great generals, it is also an elaborate portrait of the American people—individuals and families, northerners and southerners, soldiers and civilians, slaves and slaveholders, rich and poor, urban and rural, caught up in the turbulence of the times.

Jim Crow, Segregation and Violence

In the late 1860s and early 1870s, white southerners waged a war of intimidation and terror against African Americans through racist organizations like the Ku Klux Klan. This lawlessness was coupled with laws that deprived African Americans of any human rights. In 1877, President Rutherford B. Hayes brought an end to the progress African Americans had made under the Reconstruction laws.

Jim Crow laws restricted African Americans to inferior education, housing and employment opportunities. More important, these laws denied them the right to vote. Southerners resorted to mob terror, lynchings, race riots and the destruction of stable black communities. From the 1870s through the 1950s, African Americans were beaten, maimed, tortured and killed. In response, African Americans took a stand against segregation, lynching and mob violence. Many black leaders stood at the vanguard, including Ida B. Wells and Walter White. African American resistance to Jim Crow and segregation paved the way for the struggle for Civil Rights.

Without Sanctuary: Lynching Photography in America
Allen, James, ed.
Twin Palms Publishers, 212 pgs., 2000, $60.00
ISBN 0944092691

Through all the terror and carnage, someone, many times a professional photographer, carried a camera and took pictures. These lynching photographs were often made into postcards and sold as souvenirs to the crowds in attendance. James Allen traveled the country collecting these photographs.

Negrophobia: A Race Riot in Atlanta, 1906
Bauerlein, Mark
Encounter Books, 300 pgs., 2002, $16.95
ISBN 1893554546

Atlanta's dream of escaping the haunting memory of civil war and human bondage was shattered in 1906 when, in the middle of a bitter gubernatorial contest, Georgia politicians played the race card and white supremacist newspapers trumpeted a "negro crime" scare. Atlanta slipped into a climate of race hatred and sexual hysteria, culminating in a bloody riot that left over a dozen dead. Historian Mark Bauerlein traces the origins, development and brutal climax of Atlanta's descent into hatred and violence in the fateful summer of 1906.

Remembering Jim Crow: African Americans Tell About Life in the Segregated South
Chafe, William Henry, ed.
The New Press, Boxed set with CD, 346 pgs., 2001, $55.00
ISBN 1565846974
The New Press, Paperback, 384 pgs., 2003, $16.95
ISBN 1565847784

Remembering Jim Crow is the sequel to the award-winning *Remembering Slavery* (see "Slave Narratives"). Here is an extraordinary opportunity to read and hear the voices of black southerners who witnessed one of the most heartbreaking and troubling chapters in America's history. This remarkable book and CD set presents for the first time the most extensive oral history ever recorded of African American life in the racially segregated South.

LIKE JUDGMENT DAY: THE RUIN AND REDEMPTION OF A TOWN CALLED ROSEWOOD
D'Orso, Michael
Berkley Publishing Group, 384 pgs., 1996, $12.00
ISBN 1572972564

Like Judgment Day is the true story of the ruin and redemption of a town called Rosewood, where, on New Year's Day 1923, a white mob descended, burning houses, killing uncounted numbers of black men and women, and driving the rest of the inhabitants away forever. For over seventy years the events in Rosewood remained buried, the truth unacknowledged.

JIM CROW'S CHILDREN
Irons, Peter
Viking Press, 400 pgs., 2002, $29.95
ISBN 0670889180

In 1954 the U.S. Supreme Court sounded the death knell for school segregation with its decision in *Brown* v. *Board of Education of Topeka*. Yet today, writes historian Peter Irons, many U.S. schools are even more segregated than they were on the day when Brown was decided. In *Jim Crow's Children*, Irons paints vivid portraits of lawyers and judges—among them Thurgood Marshall, John W. Davis, Felix Frankfurter and Earl Warren—as well as captivating sketches of black children—like Sarah Roberts in 1849, Linda Brown in 1954 and Kalima Jenkins in 1995—whose parents joined lawsuits against Jim Crow schools.

THE PROMISED LAND: THE GREAT BLACK MIGRATION AND HOW IT CHANGED AMERICA
Lemann, Nicholas
Vintage, 416 pgs., 1992, $16.00
ISBN 0679733477

This is the definitive history of the migration of African

Americans from the rural South to the urban North. In chronicling the post-1940 northward migration of blacks, Lemann examines the poverty programs of the Kennedy, Johnson and Nixon administrations, as well as the Daley political machine. The book is framed around accounts of three people who make their way from the Mississippi Delta to Chicago—a schoolteacher turned civil servant, a storefront preacher and an elderly woman named Ruby Haynes.

The Burning: Massacre, Destruction, and the Tulsa Race Riot of 1921
Madigan, Tim
Griffin Trade Paperback, 336 pgs., 2003, $13.95
ISBN 0312302479

On the morning of June 1, 1921, a white mob numbering in the thousands marched across the railroad tracks dividing black from white in Tulsa, Oklahoma. A black community then known as the Negro Wall Street of America was reduced to smoldering rubble. *The Burning* re-creates the town of Greenwood at the height of its prosperity; explores the currents of hatred, racism and mistrust between Tulsa's black residents and the neighboring white population; recounts the events leading up to and including the holocaust at Greenwood. Finally, it documents the subsequent silence that surrounded the tragedy.

A Lynching in the Heartland: Race and Memory in America
Madison, James H.
Palgrave Macmillan, 240 pgs., 2003, $15.95
ISBN 1403961212

Historian James H. Madison has put Marian, Indiana, under the microscope and written an anatomy of a lynching. There were to be three black youths hanged that night, but divine providence spared one, James Cameron. Madison reveals that blacks didn't stand by idly and silently. They protested and worked tirelessly to identify the mob leaders, which resulted in seven arrests, and attended court to see justice served. Not only did they protest, black men stood armed and ready to defend James Cameron when he was given a sentence of two to ten years in the Indiana State Reformatory. (See *A Time of Terror* in "Autobiography.")

LET NOBODY TURN US AROUND: VOICES OF RESISTANCE, REFORM, AND RENEWAL
Marable, Manning, and Leith Mullings, eds.
Rowman and Littlefield, 704 pgs., 1999, $35.00
ISBN 0847699307

This anthology of black writers traces the evolution of African American perspectives throughout American history, from the early years of slavery to the end of the twentieth century. The essays, manifestos, interviews and documents assembled here, contextualized with critical commentaries from Marable and Mullings, introduce the reader to the character and important controversies of each period of black history.

THE LYNCHING OF EMMETT TILL: A DOCUMENTARY NARRATIVE
Metress, Christopher, ed.
University Press of Virginia, 384 pgs., 2002, $18.95
ISBN 0813921228

At 2:00 A.M. on August 28, 1955, fourteen-year-old Emmett Till, visiting from Chicago, was accused of whistling at a white woman shopkeeper. Till was abducted from his great-uncle's cabin in Money, Mississippi, and never seen alive again. His battered and bloated corpse floated to the surface of the Tallahatchie River three days later and two local white men were arrested, but never convicted, for his murder. Till's death was one of the sparks that set off the Civil Rights movement.

AMERICAN NIGHTMARE: THE HISTORY OF JIM CROW
Packard, Jerrold M.
St. Martin's Press, 304 pgs., 2003, $14.95
ISBN 031230241X

In this work, historian Jerrold M. Packard examines the laws and customs known as Jim Crow. For the hundred years following the end of the Civil War, a quarter of all Americans lived under this system of legalized segregation. Together with its rigidly enforced canon of racial "etiquette," these rules governed nearly every aspect of life as well as outlined the draconian punishments for infractions.

Southern Horrors and Other Writings: The Anti-Lynching Campaign of Ida B. Wells, 1892–1900
Wells, Ida B., edited by Jacqueline Royster
Bedford Books, 228 pgs., 1996, $14.95
ISBN 0312116950

This brief volume introduces readers to the prominent reformer and journalist Ida B. Wells and her late-nineteenth-century crusade to abolish lynching. Built around three crucial documents—Wells's pamphlet "Southern Horrors" (1892), her essay "A Red Record" (1895) and her case study "Mob Rule in New Orleans" (1900)—the volume shows how Wells defined lynching for an international audience as an issue deserving public concern and action. The editor's introduction places lynching in its historical context and provides important background information on Wells's life and career.

Rope and Faggot: A Biography of Judge Lynch
White, Walter
University of Notre Dame Press, 312 pgs., 2002, $23.95
ISBN 0268040079

In 1926, Walter White, assistant secretary of the National Association for the Advancement of Colored People, broke the story of a horrific lynching in Aiken, South Carolina, in which three African Americans were murdered while more than one thousand people watched. Because of his light complexion, blond hair and blue eyes, White, an African American, was able to investigate firsthand more than forty lynchings and eight race riots.

THE CIVIL RIGHTS MOVEMENT

Jim Crow and segregation defined the next step in the struggle for equality for African Americans. There was massive resistance to segregation laws that denied African Americans the same rights as whites. Black resistance took shape in the form of lawsuits, sit-ins, marches and protests. White resistance took shape in the form of mortgage foreclosures on black homes, loss of jobs, banks refusing loans to black borrowers and more violence.

The movement against segregation grew from grassroots organizations to national organizations such as the National Association for the Advancement of Colored People (NAACP), the Student Nonviolent Coordinating Committee (SNCC) and the National Urban League. Many figures rose to prominence as leaders of the Civil Rights movement, including Mary Church Terrell, Ralph Bunche, Roy Wilkerson, Martin Luther King Jr. and Rosa Parks.

PARTING THE WATERS: AMERICA IN THE KING YEARS, 1954–1965

Branch, Taylor
Simon & Schuster, 1,088 pgs., 1989, $20.00
ISBN 0671687425

Moving from the fiery political baptism of Martin Luther King Jr. to the corridors of Camelot where the Kennedy brothers weighed demands for justice against the deceptions of J. Edgar Hoover, here is a vivid tapestry of America, torn and finally transformed by a revolutionary struggle unequaled since the Civil War. In *Parting the Waters*, Taylor Branch provides a portrait of King's rise to greatness and illuminates the stunning courage and private conflict, the deals, maneuvers, betrayals and rivalries that determined history behind closed doors, at boycotts and sit-ins, on bloody freedom rides and through siege and murder.

THE EYES ON THE PRIZE: CIVIL RIGHTS READER: DOCUMENTS, SPEECHES, AND FIRSTHAND ACCOUNTS FROM THE BLACK FREEDOM STRUGGLE

Carson, Clayborne, ed.
Penguin USA, 784 pgs., 1991, $18.00
ISBN 0140154035

The Eyes on the Prize: Civil Rights Reader is a record of one of the greatest and most turbulent movements of the twentieth century. This is essential reading for anyone interested in learning how far the Civil Rights movement has come and how far it has yet to go. Included are the Supreme Court's *Brown v. Board of Education* decision in its entirety; speeches by Martin Luther King Jr. and his famous "Letter from a Birmingham City Jail"; an interview with Rosa Parks; selections from *Malcolm X Speaks* and much more.

MY SOUL IS A WITNESS: A CHRONOLOGY OF THE CIVIL RIGHTS ERA, 1954–1965

Collier-Thomas, Bettye, and V. P. Franklin, eds.
Henry Holt, 268 pgs., 2000, $30.00
ISBN 0805047697

Although Martin Luther King Jr. was a towering figure during the era, the authors shift the focus to the thousands of people, places and events that encompassed the Civil Rights movement. Each entry is based on information found in articles and reports published in three newspaper and periodical sources: *The New York Times*, *Jet Magazine* and the *Southern School News*.

VOICES OF FREEDOM: AN ORAL HISTORY FROM THE 1950S THROUGH THE 1980S
Hampton, Henry
Bantam Books, 692 pgs., 1991, $22.95
ISBN 0553352326

In this monumental volume, filmmaker Henry Hampton, creator and executive producer of the acclaimed PBS series *Eyes on the Prize*, draws upon nearly one thousand interviews with civil rights activists, politicians, reporters, Justice Department officials and hundreds of ordinary people who took part in the struggle, weaving a fascinating narrative of the Civil Rights movement told by the people who lived it.

THERE IS A RIVER: THE BLACK STRUGGLE FOR FREEDOM IN AMERICA
Harding, Vincent
Harcourt, 401 pgs., 1992, $17.00
ISBN 0156890895

A great black river surges in opposition to the powerful currents of slavery and racism. The struggle began on the slave ships off the coast of West Africa, with many captives choosing to rebel or drown rather than submit to bondage. Historian Vincent Harding resurrects these forgotten heroes and follows the continuing struggle of their descendants in the New World, where resistance, fed by fierce pride and unshakable hope, assumed many forms and survived a variety of political, social and military assaults.

Why We Can't Wait
King, Martin Luther, Jr.
Signet Classic, 176 pgs., 2000, $6.95
ISBN 0451527534

In Birmingham, Alabama, in 1963, Dr. Martin Luther King Jr. demonstrated to the world the power of nonviolent direct action. *Why We Can't Wait* recounts not only the Birmingham campaign but it also examines the history of the civil rights struggle and the tasks that future generations must accomplish to bring about full equality for African Americans. Dr. King's eloquent analysis of these events propelled the Civil Rights movement from lunch-counter sit-ins and prayer marches to the forefront of the American consciousness.

The Papers of Martin Luther King, Jr.
King, Martin Luther, Jr., edited by Clayborne Carson
Vol. 1, Called to Serve, January 1929–June 1951: *University of California Press, 507 pgs., 1992, $50.00*
ISBN 0520079507
Vol. 2, Rediscovering Precious Values, July 1951–November 1955: *University of California Press, 800 pgs., 1994, $50.00*
ISBN 0520079515
Vol. 3, Birth of a New Age, December 1955–December 1956: *University of California Press, 598 pgs., 1997, $50.00*
ISBN 0520079523
Vol. 4, Symbol of the Movement, January 1957–December 1958: *University of California Press, 670 pgs., 2000, $50.00*
ISBN 0520222318

Martin Luther King Jr.'s ideas, his call for racial equality, his faith in the ultimate triumph of justice and his insistence on the power of nonviolent struggle to bring about a major transformation of American society are as vital and timely as ever. His writings, both published and unpublished, which constitute his intellectual legacy, are now preserved in this authoritative, chronologically arranged, multivolume edition. Faithfully transcribing the texts of his letters, speeches, sermons, student papers and articles, this series has no equal. *The Papers of Martin Luther*

King, Jr. is a testament to a man whose life and teaching continue to have a profound influence not only on Americans but on people of all nations.

WALKING WITH THE WIND: A MEMOIR OF THE MOVEMENT
Lewis, John, and Michael D'Orso
Harcourt, 496 pgs., 1999, $16.00
ISBN 0156007088

The son of an Alabama sharecropper, and now a nine-term U.S. congressman, John Lewis has led an extraordinary life, one that found him at the epicenter of the Civil Rights movement in the late fifties and sixties. As chairman of the Student Nonviolent Coordinating Committee (SNCC), Lewis was present at all the major battlefields of the movement. Arrested more than forty times and severely beaten on several occasions, he was one of the youngest yet most courageous of the movement's leaders.

FREEDOM'S DAUGHTERS: THE UNSUNG HEROINES OF THE CIVIL RIGHTS MOVEMENT FROM 1830 TO 1970
Olson, Lynne
Scribner, 464 pgs., 2002, $16.00
ISBN 0684850133

From the Montgomery bus boycott to the lunch-counter sit-ins to the Freedom Rides, Lynne Olson skillfully tells the long-overlooked story of the extraordinary women who were among the most fearless, resourceful and tenacious leaders of the Civil Rights movement. *Freedom's Daughters* includes portraits of more than sixty women—many until now forgotten and some never before written about—from the key figures (Ida B. Wells, Eleanor Roosevelt, Ella Baker and Septima Clark, among others) to some of the smaller players who represent the hundreds of women who each came forth to do her own small part and who together ultimately formed the mass movements that made the difference.

EYES ON THE PRIZE: AMERICA'S CIVIL RIGHTS YEARS, 1954–1965

Williams, Juan
Penguin USA, 320 pgs., 1988, $18.00
ISBN 0140096531

From the Montgomery bus boycott to the Little Rock Nine to the Selma-Montgomery march, thousands of ordinary people made up the American Civil Rights movement. *Eyes on the Prize* tells the story of these people. From leaders like Martin Luther King Jr. to lesser-known participants like Barbara Rose Johns and Jim Awerg, each man and woman made the decision that discrimination was wrong and that something had to be done to stop it. This book is the companion volume to the PBS TV series of the same name.

THE BLACK POWER MOVEMENT

The Civil Rights era addressed many of the ills in American society, but younger blacks took a bolder step in confronting racism in the mid-sixties with a new black consciousness of racial pride and self-empowerment. This movement also fostered in the younger, more militant blacks a new sense of responsibility for defending their communities and neighborhoods. Black Power became synonymous with a return to African culture and sensibilities, economic and political empowerment and the right to an African-centered worldview.

Most whites and some blacks, including the NAACP, rejected the existence of organizations like the Black Panther Party, which took root in urban communities. Separatist, antiestablishment views and rhetoric fostered the notion that the Black Power movement was antiwhite. What the Black Power movement wanted was revolutionary action to overcome the racist and imperialistic policies of the United States. The U.S. government reacted with infiltrators and spies, causing the eventual dissolution of the party. However, the cultural-nationalist influence on the arts continues to be a source of inspiration today.

A Taste of Power: A Black Woman's Story
Brown, Elaine
Anchor Books, 452 pgs., 1994, $16.95
ISBN 0385471076

In August 1974, Elaine Brown proclaimed to the assembled leadership of the Black Panther Party that she was now in charge. The Panthers had grown from a small Oakland-based cell to a national organization that had mobilized black communities throughout the country. Huey Newton, heading for refuge in Cuba, asked Elaine Brown to hold together a party threatened by internal conflict and the FBI. More than a journey through a turbulent time in American history, *A Taste of Power* is the story of a black woman's battle to define herself—how she reached her position of power over a paramilitary, male-dominated organization and what she did with that power is an unsparing story of self-discovery.

Soul on Ice
Cleaver, Eldridge
Delta Publishing, 224 pgs., 1999, $13.95
ISBN 038533379X

First published in 1954, when he was eighteen years old and imprisoned on rape and marijuana charges, Eldridge Cleaver's brutally honest autobiography shocked America.

Sisters in the Struggle: African-American Women in the Civil Rights and Black Power Movements
Collier-Thomas, Bettye, and V. P. Franklin, eds.
New York University Press, 400 pgs., 2001, $20.00
ISBN 0814716032

Sisters in the Struggle tells the stories and documents the contributions of African American women to the most important social reform movements in the United States in the twentieth century. Only recently have historians and other researchers begun to recognize black women's central role in the battle for racial and gender equality. It also includes personal testimonies from women like Rosa Parks, Charlayne Hunter Gault and Dorothy Height, who made headlines with their courageous resistance to racism and sexism.

THE HUEY P. NEWTON READER
Hilliard, David, ed.
Seven Stories Press, 480 pgs., 2002, $17.95
ISBN 158322467X

Beginning with his founding of the Black Panther Party in 1966, Huey Newton set the political stage for events that would place him and the Panthers at the forefront of the African American liberation movement for the next twenty years. *The Huey P. Newton Reader* includes now-classic texts ranging from the formation of the Black Panthers, the arming of young urban blacks for self-defense and Eldridge Cleaver's controversial expulsion from the party to FBI infiltration of Civil Rights groups, the Vietnam War and the burgeoning feminist movement.

THIS SIDE OF GLORY: THE AUTOBIOGRAPHY OF DAVID HILLIARD AND THE STORY OF THE BLACK PANTHER PARTY
Hilliard, David, and Lewis Cole
Lawrence Hill and Co., 480 pgs., 2001, $18.95
ISBN 155652384X

David Hilliard was the chief of staff of the Black Panther Party. This is his compelling eyewitness account of America's first black armed revolutionary movement. Written with the participation of many other party members, this book provides firsthand accounts of Huey Newton's infamous shootout with the police, the murder of Fred Hampton, how Panther money was raised and spent, the sexual mores of the party and how illegal activities erupted and were controlled. According to the FBI, the Panthers were "the greatest threat to the internal security of the country." In part due to government infiltrators and disinformation, the party began to dissolve in the early seventies as police raids, gun battles, IRS investigations, trials and prison terms decimated their ranks.

BLACK POWER: THE POLITICS OF LIBERATION IN AMERICA
Ture, Kwame, and Charles V. Hamilton
Vintage, 230 pgs., 1992, $13.00
ISBN 0679743138

In 1967, Stokely Carmichael (Kwame Ture) and Charles V. Hamilton exposed the depths of systemic racism in this country and provided a radical political framework for reform. African Americans could no longer believe that their liberation would come through traditional political processes: True and lasting social change would be accomplished only through unity among African Americans and their independence from the preexisting order. The authors offer unflinching assessments of the tenets of Black Power as they have or have not been realized and reassert the urgency of addressing the liberation struggles of Africans all over the world.

NEW DAY IN BABYLON: THE BLACK POWER MOVEMENT AND AMERICAN CULTURE, 1965–1975
Van Deburg, William L.
University of Chicago Press, 378 pgs., 1992, $18.00
ISBN 0226847152

William Van Deburg has written a comprehensive account of the rise and fall of the Black Power movement and of its dramatic transformation of both African American and the larger American culture. *New Day in Babylon* chronicles a decade of deep change, from the armed struggles of the Black Panther Party and the separatism of the Nation of Islam to the cultural nationalism of artists and writers creating a new black aesthetic.

AMERICAN RACISM

Racism is an institutionalized system of denial based on race and ethnicity. American history begins with the near extermination of America's native population. Throughout American history racism has been practiced against African Americans in the form of slavery, violence, denial of medical services and police brutality. These kinds of racist practices have been documented and are undeniable. However, there are other forms of racism that are much more subtle. For example: Racism is a part of the educational system of America, due to the failure of local governments to make educational opportunities available to all children. There are racist real estate practices designed to keep people of color from certain areas. The legal system of America is another bastion of racism, with disparate sentencing systems and racial profiling working against people of color, especially African Americans. Racism is ingrained in the fabric of American society and will most likely stay that way to the detriment of all Americans.

BREAKING THE CHAINS OF PSYCHOLOGICAL SLAVERY
Akbar, Na'im
Mind Productions, 95 pgs., 1999, $10.00
ISBN 0935257055

Are African Americans still slaves? Why can't black folks get together? What is the psychological consequence for blacks and whites of picturing God as a Caucasian? Akbar presents a penetrating and concise analysis of slavery and racial religious images on the psychological functioning of African Americans. This book reveals the psychological chains of slavery and presents some helpful suggestions for breaking the chains.

FACES AT THE BOTTOM OF THE WELL:
THE PERMANENCE OF RACISM
Bell, Derrick A.
Basic Books, 240 pgs., 1993, $15.00
ISBN 0465068146

Professor Derrick Bell drives home his point through a series of allegorical stories and encounters with fictional characters. The book sends a sobering message: Racism is so integral a part of American life that no matter what blacks do to better their lot, they are doomed to fail as long as the majority of whites do not see that their own well-being is threatened by the inferior status of blacks. Bell calls on blacks to face up to this unhappy truth and abandon the misleading vision of "we shall overcome."

THE CONDEMNATION OF LITTLE B.
Brown, Elaine
Beacon Press, 391 pgs., 2003, $19.00
ISBN 080700975X

Through the story of a thirteen-year-old black boy condemned to life in prison, Elaine Brown exposes the "New Age" racism that effectively condemns millions of poor African Americans to a third-world life. The story of "Little B" is a riveting, stunning example of the particular burden racism imposes on black youths. Most astonishing, almost all of the officials involved in bringing "Little B" to "justice" are black.

RACE RULES: NAVIGATING THE COLOR LINE
Dyson, Michael Eric
Vintage, 256 pgs., 1997, $12.00
ISBN 0679781560

From the O. J. Simpson trial to the generational politics of gangsta rap, and from Colin Powell to Louis Farrakhan, Dyson takes on the most contentious issues of the 1990s. Again and again he shows us that, in a society that prides itself on being color-blind, race is more important—and more pernicious—than ever.

TWO NATIONS: SEPARATE, HOSTILE, UNEQUAL
Hacker, Andrew
Ballantine Books, 283 pgs., 1995, $12.95
ISBN 0345405374

In his analysis of a divided society, Political Science professor Andrew Hacker explains why racial disparities persist. This startling look at the facts that so many choose to ignore is balanced by the voices of African Americans. Hacker shows how race influences the attitudes and behavior of all Americans.

BAD BLOOD: THE TUSKEGEE SYPHILIS EXPERIMENT
Jones, James H.
Free Press, 297 pgs., 1993, $17.95
ISBN 0029166764

The U.S. Public Health system decided to let the syphilis affecting a group of black sharecroppers take its course without treatment. This account explains how such a tragedy could occur.

POLICE BRUTALITY: AN ANTHOLOGY
Nelson, Jill, ed.
W.W. Norton, 320 pgs., 2001, $14.95
ISBN 0393321630

In recent years, nothing has blotted the American imagination so starkly as the highway beating of Rodney King, the shooting of the unarmed and innocent Amadou Diallo and the savage torture of Abner Louima in a Brooklyn police precinct bathroom. Jill Nelson offers an anthology of thirteen essays by writers as varied as historian Robin G. Kelley, law professor Derrick Bell, retired New York Police Department Lieutenant Arthur Doyle, and criminologist Katheryn K. Russell.

A Death in Texas: A Story of Race, Murder, and a Small Town's Struggle for Redemption
Temple-Raston, Dina
Owl Books, 352 pgs., 2003, $15.00
ISBN 0805072772

Before 1998 few Americans had ever heard of Jasper, Texas. That all changed on June 7, 1998, when a trio of young white men chained a forty-nine-year-old black man named James Byrd Jr. to the bumper of a truck and dragged him three miles down a country road. From the initial investigation through the trials and their aftermath, *A Death in Texas* follows the turn of events through the eyes of Billy Rowles, an enlightened lawman determined to take lessons from the tragedy, and other townspeople trying to come to grips with the brutal killing.

The Isis Papers: The Keys to the Colors
Welsing, Frances Cress
Third World Press, 300 pgs., 1991, $16.95
ISBN 0883781042

Dr. Welsing offers eye-opening and controversial theories with regards to the origin and perpetuation of racism. *The Isis Papers* is a compilation of her lectures and papers over the course of more than thirty years.

The Mis-education of the Negro
Woodson, Carter, edited by Jawanza Kunjufu
African American Images, 240 pgs., 2000, $9.50
ISBN 0913543705

Originally published in 1933, *The Mis-education of the Negro* continues to resonate today. The impact of slavery on the black psyche is explored and questions are raised about the American education system. Woodson takes a different approach to education, requiring more study, discipline and an Africentric worldview. This new edition contains a biographical profile of the author, a new introduction and study questions.

FICTION

While fiction often contains many elements of real life, the story is made up—all in the author's mind. Through fiction, an author is able to put the most incredible thoughts and ideas together to weave a story. Fiction invites you to suspend disbelief and travel to fantastic places under incredible circumstances.

Fiction is an important element in the African American library. Some of our most notable African American writers have created classical works in this form, among them Toni Morrison, Ernest Gaines, Alice Walker and John Edgar Wideman—to name a few. Their works of fiction have been read and reread for many years. But there are also many writers of whom you may not have heard, such as Opal Palmer Adisa and Colson Whitehead. Their works have a timeless quality and allow you to experience times and circumstances beyond your own experiences. That's where I come in.

The fictional works I list here have a strength and beauty that will stand for hundreds of years to come. Each new reader will experience the joys and struggles right along with the characters. They will become a part of your life. You may find yourself thinking about them long after you've read the last word. You may remember a passage or a particular scene and find yourself smiling or maybe frowning. That's what a good work of fiction can do.

COLONIAL LITERATURE
(1746–1900)

The African American literary tradition began in the mid-eighteenth century with the publication of slave narratives. The earliest colonial authors wrote about themselves in fictionalized stories, and also created characters that bore no resemblance to them. Their stories of servitude and ill treatment at the hands of white people are often contrasted with their stories of how they were also mistreated by other blacks.

One prevailing theme of these earliest writers was the practice of black people "passing" for white. Among the earliest female writers, some wrote of love and relationships in the romantic style of the times. While these stories may seem tame by comparison to contemporary works, they are full of emotion and drama.

Clotel: Or, the President's Daughter
Brown, William Wells, edited by Robert S. Levine
Bedford/St. Martin's, 527 pgs., 2000, $12.10
ISBN 0312152655

First published in 1853, *Clotel* tells the story, in circulation at the time, that Thomas Jefferson fathered an illegitimate mulatto daughter who was sold into slavery. Brown's story puts Jefferson in place as the father of two daughters born to a slave named Currer. Powerfully reimagining this story, and weaving together a variety of contemporary source materials, Brown fills the novel with daring escapes and encounters, as well as searing depictions of the American slave trade.

The Conjure Woman and Other Conjure Tales
Chesnutt, Charles W., edited by Richard H. Brodhead
Duke University Press, 207 pgs., 1993, $15.95
ISBN 0822313871

This edition reassembles for the first time all of Charles W. Chesnutt's 1899 work in the conjure tale genre. It also allows the reader to see how the published volume was created, how an African American author negotiated with tastes of the dominant literary culture of the late-nineteenth century.

The Bondwoman's Narrative
Crafts, Hannah, edited by Henry Louis Gates Jr.
Warner Books, 464 pgs., 2002, $14.95
ISBN 0446690295

This tale, written in the 1850s, is the only known novel by a female African American fugitive slave, and is quite possibly the first novel written by a black woman anywhere. It is a stirring, page-turning story of "passing" and the adventures of a young slave as she makes her way to freedom. Presented here unaltered and under its author's original title, *The Bondwoman's Narrative* tells of a self-educated young house slave who knows her life is limited by the brutalities of her society, but never suspects that the freedom of her plantation's beautiful new mistress is also at risk.

FICTION

BLAKE; OR, THE HUTS OF AMERICA
Delaney, Martin R.
Beacon Press, 1989, $20.00
ISBN 080706419X

Martin R. Delaney has been called the father of American black nationalism. His only novel, *Blake*, originally published in serial form in 1861–62, powerfully dramatizes his separatist philosophy. Delaney's hero is a West Indian slave who travels throughout the South advocating revolution and later becomes the general of a black insurrectionary force in Cuba.

MINNIE'S SACRIFICE, SOWING AND REAPING, TRIAL AND TRIUMPH: THREE REDISCOVERED NOVELS
Harper, Frances E. W., edited by Francis Smith Foster
Beacon Press, 304 pgs., 2000, $14.00
ISBN 0807062332

In one of the most significant literary finds since the publication of Harriet Wilson's *Our Nig*, Frances Smith Foster has rediscovered three novels by Frances E. W. Harper, the best-known African American woman writer of the nineteenth century. Originally serialized in issues of *The Christian Recorder* between 1868 and 1888, these works are the first written specifically for an African American audience. The heroine of *Minnie's Sacrifice* must weigh the social benefits of passing for white against her desire to join the African American struggle for equality and justice. *Sowing and Reaping* focuses on the issue of temperance, while domestic issues of courtship and marriage form the basis for *Trial and Triumph*, a lively drama about finding a suitable mate. These novels shed light on the lives of nineteenth-century African Americans.

"LE MULATRE/THE MULATTO"
Séjour, Victor, edited by Henry Louis Gates Jr.
Norton Anthology of African American Literature, pgs. 286–99
W.W. Norton, 1997, $59.75
ISBN 0393959082

First African American short story, published in France in

1837, "Le Mulatre" is about a mulatto slave who kills his white father.

OUR NIG; OR, SKETCHES FROM THE LIFE OF A FREE BLACK

Wilson, Harriet E., edited by Henry Louis Gates Jr.
Vintage, 288 pgs., 2002, $12.00
ISBN 1400031206

The story begins with six-year-old Frado, deserted by her white mother after the death of her black father and left to live as a servant to a white family in Massachusetts. Frado is treated like a slave by the mistress of the house and by her daughter. Once considered to be the first book written by an African American woman, *Our Nig* is a deeply ironic and highly readable work.

The Harlem Renaissance
(1917–1940)

After World War I, African American genius and creativity was at the forefront of American culture. Harlem became the "capital" of black America and was teeming with artists, composers, singers, poets and novelists. This was a period of intellectual and creative inspiration.

Black writers abandoned the formal styles of writing associated with classical European literary traditions and began to speak out in their own voices. Themes of racial pride and identity, gender and sexuality, politics and race relations began to emerge. The Harlem Renaissance produced writers like Dorothy West, James Baldwin, Arna Bontemps, Jean Toomer, Nella Larsen and Jessie Redmon Fauset. For the first time in history, America took African American literature and the arts seriously.

THERE IS CONFUSION
Fauset, Jessie Redmon
Northeastern University Press, 297 pgs., 1989, $17.95
ISBN 1555530664

This first novel, written in 1924 by the author of *Plum Bun and the Chinaberry Tree*, shows an awareness of the black middle class's quest for social equality in the early years of the twentieth century and, in particular, of the choices confronting black women in the urban North. Set in Philadelphia, *There Is Confusion* traces the lives of Joanna Marshall and Peter Bye, two people whose families must come to terms with an inheritance of prejudice and discrimination as they struggle for legitimacy and respect.

NOT WITHOUT LAUGHTER
Hughes, Langston, edited by Maya Angelou
Scribner, 304 pgs., 1995, $12.00
ISBN 0020209851

Langston Hughes was one of the best-known poets in modern America and his first novel, *Not Without Laughter*, is undoubtedly his finest prose. A classic of African American literature, it is the poignant story of a young black boy's awakening to the sad and beautiful realities of black life in a small Kansas town. Originally published in 1930, *Not Without Laughter* is a pioneering work of fiction and has been in print ever since.

THEIR EYES WERE WATCHING GOD
Hurston, Zora Neale
Harper Perennial Classics, 240 pgs., 1999, $13.95
ISBN 0060931418

This novel about a proud, independent black woman was first published in 1937 and generally dismissed by reviewers. *Their Eyes Were Watching God* tells the story of Janie Crawford, a fair-skinned, long-haired, dreamy woman who comes of age expecting better treatment than what she gets from her three husbands and community. Then she meets Tea Cake, a younger man who captivates her heart and spirit, and offers her the chance to relish life without being one man's mule or another man's adornment.

MR. POTTER
Kincaid, Jamaica
Farrar, Straus and Giroux, 208 pgs., 2003, $12.00
ISBN 0374528748

Jamaica Kincaid's first obsession, the island of Antigua, comes vibrantly to life under the gaze of Mr. Potter, an illiterate chauffeur who makes his living along the wide, open roads that pass the only towns he has ever seen and the graveyard where he will be buried. Kincaid introduces us to Mr. Potter's ancestors—beginning with his father, a poor fisherman, and his mother, who committed suicide—and the refugees fleeing the collapsing world that press in on Mr. Potter's life.

MY BROTHER
Kincaid, Jamaica
Farrar, Straus and Giroux, 208 pgs., 1998, $11.00
ISBN 0374216819

Jamaica Kincaid's brother Devon Drew died of AIDS on January 19, 1996, at the age of thirty-three. A dreamer who aroused both love and anger, he died painfully and alone in his mother's house. Kincaid's often shockingly frank recounting of her brother's life is also the story of her family on the island of Antigua, centered on the powerful, sometimes threatening figure of the writer's mother. Kincaid's unblinking record of a life that ended too early speaks volumes about the difficult truths at the heart of all families.

THE COMPLETE FICTION OF NELLA LARSEN
Larsen, Nella, with an introduction by Charles Larson
Anchor Books, 304 pgs., 2001, $13.00
ISBN 0385721005

Nella Larsen wrote about women who were racially and sexually oppressed, and her short story "Wrong Man," published in 1926, is a great introduction to her writing style. In "Wrong Man," a happily married woman agonizes over the appearance of a past lover. She sends him a note to meet her in a garden, where she will appeal to him to never reveal their past relationship. She pleads her case eloquently, but to the wrong man. Larsen's critically acclaimed novel, *Quicksand*, first published in 1928, is more of an autobiography than a work of fiction. Helga Crane was trapped in her own middle-class black hell, unhappy being neither black nor white. She was unhappy in America, in Harlem and finally in Denmark. Larsen's third novel, *Passing*, published in 1929, is a haunting and chilling story of friends divided by destiny. Irene Redfield is haunted by the secret of knowing that her childhood friend Clare Kendry is passing for white. Clare's husband refers to his wife as "Nig" because she appears to be darkening with age.

THE PORTABLE HARLEM RENAISSANCE READER
Lewis, David Levering, ed.
Penguin USA, 770 pgs., 1995, $17.00
ISBN 0140170367

The Portable Renaissance Reader includes the work of some forty-five Renaissance figures. Alongside some of the most famous literary creations of the era appear unusual and previously unpublished material such as Paul Robeson's reflections on *The Emperor Jones* and Aaron Douglas's recounting of the painting of his monumental Fiske mural.

HOME TO HARLEM
McKay, Claude
Northeastern University Press, 340 pgs., 1987, $15.95
ISBN 1555530249

Jake is on the run. After serving overseas with the U.S. Army, he goes AWOL and makes his way back home to Harlem. Back to the life he had before. Back to the basement joints, pool rooms and rent parties. But no hero's welcome awaits him. Only the same hard-drinking, hard-living scrabble for love and a home that he left behind. In this world of gamblers, loan sharks, lonely women and rivals in love, Jake seems to have it all. But the women of Harlem aren't the only ones keen to make this fine-looking soldier their man. Uncle Sam wants him, too! Written in 1928, McKay's 1920s Harlem is very different from Harlem in the twenty-first century.

CANE
Toomer, Jean
Liveright Publishing, 144 pgs., 1993, $11.95
ISBN 0871401517

A literary masterpiece of the Harlem Renaissance, *Cane*, written in 1923, is a powerful work of innovative fiction evoking black life in the South. The sketches, poems and stories of black rural and urban life that make up *Cane* are rich in imagery. Visions of smoke, sugarcane, dusk and flame permeate the southern landscape while the northern world is pictured as a harsh reality of asphalt streets. Impressionistic, sometimes surrealistic, the pieces are redolent of nature and Africa, with sensuous appeal to eye and ear.

THE FIRE IN THE FLINT: A YOUNG DOCTOR'S TRAGIC CONFRONTATION WITH THE SEGREGATED SOUTH
White, Walter F.
University of Georgia Press, 312 pgs., 1995, $19.95
ISBN 082031742X

Written in 1924 by a lifelong champion of civil rights, this is the story of Kenneth Harper, a young black physician who, after having studied in the North in the early part of the twentieth century, returns to his hometown of Central City in south Georgia to practice medicine. Believing the days of oppression for blacks in the South were waning, Harper finds all too soon that the roots of intolerance run deep. As he becomes increasingly aware of the ways in which the black community remains enslaved, Harper helps local sharecroppers organize a cooperative society to share in the economic freedom traditionally reserved for white landowners. The Ku Klux Klan is quickly rallied into action, and Harper finds himself in a violent and vengeful battle with the Klan. Amid the story's tragedy and violence, Walter White reflects the complex nuances of humanity within white and black communities in conflict.

POST–HARLEM RENAISSANCE
(1940–1980)

The Harlem Renaissance opened the way for African American writers to explore the conditions and lifestyles of blacks in their environments. Authors began to write about the cities in greater detail. Writers such as Ralph Ellison began to explore the themes of the alienation, isolation and invisibility of the black American. Southern writers such as Ernest Gaines wrote about life for southern blacks under Jim Crow and segregation. Women writers began to explore themes of sexism, racism, sexual and domestic violence, abandonment and single motherhood. The works became much more realistic and closer to the everyday lives of black Americans.

If Beale Street Could Talk
Baldwin, James
Bantam Doubleday, 177 pgs., 1985, $6.99
ISBN 0440340608

Like the blues—sweet, sad and full of truth—this masterly work of fiction written in 1974, rocks us with powerful emotions. In it are anger and pain, but above all love—the affirmative love of a woman for her man, the sustaining love of a black family. Fonny, a talented young artist, finds himself unjustly arrested and locked in New York's infamous Tombs. But his girlfriend, Tish, is determined to free him, and to have his baby.

Gorilla, My Love
Bambara, Toni Cade
Vintage, 177 pgs., 1992, $11.00
ISBN 0679738983

In these fifteen superb stories Toni Cade Bambara gives us a wide range of unforgettable characters in scenes shifting between uptown New York and rural North Carolina. A young girl suffers her first betrayal. A widow flirts with an elderly blind man against the wishes of her grown-up children. A neighborhood loan shark teaches a white social worker a lesson in responsibility. First published in 1972, these and more are written in Bambara's honest and down-to-earth style.

Invisible Man
Ellison, Ralph
Vintage, 581 pgs., 1995, $12.95
ISBN 0679732764

Invisible Man is a milestone in American literature and has engaged readers since its appearance in 1952. A first novel by an unknown writer, it remained on the best-seller list for sixteen weeks, won the National Book Award for fiction and established Ralph Ellison as one of the key writers of the century. In the novel, the nameless narrator describes growing up in a black community in the South, attending a Negro college from which he is expelled, moving to New York and becoming the chief spokesman of the Harlem branch of "the Brotherhood" and retreating amid violence and confusion to his basement lair as the Invisible Man he imagines himself to be.

THE AUTOBIOGRAPHY OF MISS JANE PITMAN
Gaines, Ernest
Bantam Books, 272 pgs., 1982, $6.50
ISBN 0553263579

The Autobiography of Miss Jane Pitman is a novel in the guise of the tape-recorded recollections of a black woman who has lived 110 years, who has been both a slave and a witness to the black militancy of the 1960s. Miss Jane Pitman has "endured," has seen almost everything and foretold the rest. Gaines's novel was produced for television in 1974.

IF HE HOLLERS LET HIM GO
Himes, Chester
Thunder's Mouth Press, 216 pgs., 2002, $13.95
ISBN 1560254459

This story, of a man living every day in fear for his life simply because he's black, is as powerful today as it was when it was first published in 1947. The novel takes place in the space of four days in the life of Bob Jones, a black man who is constantly plagued by the effects of racism. Living in a society that is drenched in race consciousness has taken a toll on the way Jones behaves, thinks and feels, especially when, at the end of his story, he is accused of a brutal crime he did not commit.

THE BLUEST EYE
Morrison, Toni
Penguin USA, 216 pgs., 2000, $12.95
ISBN 0452282195

Published in 1970, Toni Morrison's first novel is the story of eleven-year-old Pecola Breedlove—a little black girl. Pecola prays for her eyes to turn blue: so that she will be beautiful, so that people will look at her, so that her world will be different. This is the story of the nightmare at the heart of her yearning and the tragedy of its fulfillment.

SONG OF SOLOMON
Morrison, Toni
Plume, 337 pgs., 1987, $14.00
ISBN 0452260116

Song of Solomon, first published in 1977, begins with one of the most arresting scenes in our century's literature: a dreamlike tableau depicting a man poised on a roof, about to fly into the air, while cloth rose petals swirl above the snow-covered ground and, in the astonished crowd below, one woman sings as another enters premature labor. The child born of that labor, Macon (Milkman) Dead, will eventually come to discover, through his complicated progress to maturity, the meaning of the drama that marked his birth.

THE WOMEN OF BREWSTER PLACE
Naylor, Gloria
Penguin USA, 192 pgs., 1983, $13.00
ISBN 014006690X

Once the home of poor Irish and Italian immigrants, Brewster Place, a rotting tenement on a dead-end street, now shelters black families. The women of Brewster Place are a community of women who have suffered in their lives but band together to better their circumstances. First published in 1977, *The Women of Brewster Place* was made into a movie for television.

THE STREET
Petry, Ann
Houghton Mifflin, 436 pgs., 1998, $12.00
ISBN 0395901499

The Street, written by Ann Petry in 1947, tells the poignant, often heartbreaking, story of Ludie Johnson, a young black woman, and her spirited struggle to raise her son amid the violence, poverty and racial dissonance of Harlem in the late 1940s.

THE FREELANCE PALLBEARERS
Reed, Ishmael
Dalkey Archive Press, 155 pgs., 1999, $11.95

ISBN 1564782255

Ishmael Reed's electrifying first novel, written in 1967, zooms readers off to a land they have never heard of, a crazy, ominous kingdom called HARRY SAM—a never-never land so weirdly out of whack that only reality itself could be stranger. Venturing into this risky realm of a thousand contradictions is the quixotic Bukka Doopeyduk, a crusading, liberal fellow who is eager, if not always ready, to face the dangers of life.

THE THIRD LIFE OF GRANGE COPELAND
Walker, Alice
Pocket Books, 352 pgs., 2000, $13.95
ISBN 0743418239

Despondent over the futility of life in the South, black tenant farmer Grange Copeland leaves his wife and son in Georgia to head north. After meeting an equally humiliating existence there, he returns to Georgia, years later, to find his son, Brownfield, imprisoned for the murder of his wife. As the guardian of the couple's youngest daughter, Grange Copeland is looking at his third and final chance to free himself from spiritual and social enslavement.

When Walker wrote this first novel in 1970, she was criticized for her negative portrayal of African American males. Walker responded to her critics by saying that she was writing from her own experience.

JUBILEE
Walker, Margaret
Houghton Mifflin, 512 pgs., 1999, $8.95
ISBN 0395924952

This stunningly different Civil War novel, written in 1966, features a heroine to rival Scarlett O'Hara of *Gone With the Wind*. Daughter of the white plantation owner and his beloved black mistress, Vyry was conceived, born and reared to womanhood behind the House. Steeped in knowledge of and feeling for the times and the people, *Jubilee* is a magnificent tale told with devastating truth.

CONTEMPORARY FICTION
(1980–2003)

At the end of the twentieth century, African American writers began to find audiences among mainstream America and gained recognition for their literary endeavors. Alice Walker won the Pulitzer Prize in 1983 for The Color Purple. *Toni Morrison became the first black woman to receive the Nobel Prize for literature. Terry McMillan's book* Waiting to Exhale *became a blockbuster hit and the publishing industry took notice, realizing that African Americans do buy and read books that they can relate to.*

Oprah Winfrey's Book Club helped bring black authors to mainstream America, giving rise to African American authors who began to self-publish. Mainstream publishers mined the fields of self-published books and gave them a wider audience through major marketing and distribution systems. African American writers broadened their horizons and began to write science fiction, fantasy and horror, as well as about sex, love and family. Contemporary African American fiction has no boundaries.

It Begins with Tears
Adisa, Opal Palmer
Heinemann, 239 pgs., 1997, $13.95
ISBN 0435989464

The seductive Monica returns to her village to make a new start. But Kristoff Village, in the heart of rural Jamaica, is about to become a whirlpool of emotion. Every encounter with Monica stirs up women's dissatisfactions and men's desires. When those emotions develop into hatred and jealousy, Monica is made to pay for what she has done.

Appalachee Red
Andrews, Raymond
University of Georgia Press, 304 pgs., 1987, $12.95
ISBN 0820309613

Bawdy and sometimes horrifying, hilarious on the way to being tragic, Raymond Andrews's Muskhogean County novel tells of black life in the Deep South from the end of the First World War to the beginning of the 1960s, from the days of mules and white men with bullwhips, to the moment when the pendulum began to swing.

Baby of the Family
Ansa, Tina McElroy
Harvest Books, 276 pgs., 1991, $13.00
ISBN 0156101505

From the moment of her birth in a rural black hospital in Georgia, Lena McPherson is recognized as a special child, with the power to see ghosts and predict the future. But only one nurse knows the spell to ensure that Lena will see good ghosts, not evil ones.

The Salt Eaters
Bambara, Toni Cade
Vintage, 295 pgs., 1992, $13.00
ISBN 0679740767

Bambara's first novel chronicling black urban life in the South through the 1950s and 1960s is set in the small town of Claybourne.

First published in 1960, *The Salt Eaters* is the story of a community of black faith healers who, searching for the healing properties of salt, witness an event that will change their lives forever.

BROTHERMAN: THE ODYSSEY OF BLACK MEN IN AMERICA
Boyd, Herb, and John L. Allen, eds.
Ballantine Books, 922 pgs., 1996, $21.95
ISBN 0345383176

Brotherman contains more than 150 selections, some never before published—slave narratives, memoirs, social histories, novels, poems, short stories, biographies, autobiographies, position papers and essays. *Brotherman* books us passage to the world that black men experience as adolescents, lovers, husbands, fathers, workers, warriors and elders.

DARKTOWN STRUTTERS
Brown, Wesley
University of Massachusetts Press, 240 pgs., 2000, $16.95
ISBN 1558492704

Darktown Strutters cuts to the cruel center of American racism. Wesley Brown's traveling minstrel show is where the symbolism of skin color establishes public meaning and private identity, the way a funhouse mirror distorts height and weight. This is a scary book, and mordantly funny, too.

WILD SEED
Butler, Octavia
Aspect, 288 pgs., 1999, $6.00
ISBN 0446606723

From African American science fiction author Octavia Butler comes number three in the Patternist series. Doro is an entity who changes bodies like clothes, killing his host by reflex or design. He fears no one, until he meets Anyanwu, who has also died many times. She fears no one, until she meets Doro. Anyanwu and Doro were the father, mother and gods of an awesome, unborn race. And their love and hate wove a pattern of destiny that not even immortals could imagine.

Your Blues Ain't Like Mine
Campbell, Bebe Moore
Ballantine Books, 433 pgs., 1995, $7.50
ISBN 0345401123

Repercussions are felt for decades in a dozen lives after a racist beating turns to cold-blooded murder in a small Mississippi town in the 1950s. Chicago-born Armstrong Todd is fifteen, black and unused to the segregated ways of the Deep South when his mother sends him to spend the summer with relatives in her native rural Mississippi. For speaking a few innocuous words in French to a white woman, Armstrong pays the ultimate price when the woman's husband, brother-in-law and father-in-law decide to teach him a lesson.

The Emperor of Ocean Park
Carter, Stephen L.
Vintage, 672 pgs., 2003, $14.00
ISBN 0375712925

Talcott Garland, a law professor at an unnamed Ivy League university, is snapped out of his private world of personal dissatisfactions by the death of his father, Judge Oliver Garland. *The Emperor of Ocean Park* is set in two privileged worlds: the upper-crust African American society of the eastern seaboard—old families who summer on Martha's Vineyard—and the inner circle of an Ivy League law school. It tells the story of a complex family with a single, seductive link to the shadowlands of crime.

The Price of a Child
Cary, Lorene
Vintage, 320 pgs., 1996, $14.00
ISBN 0679744673

In 1855, Ginne Pryor, once cook, mistress and slave to a Virginia planter, walks away from her furious master and into the embrace of a delegation of Philadelphia's Vigilance Committee. With freedom comes a new name, new pleasures and new responsibilities as she becomes a speaker on the abolition circuit. But

U.S. law still considers her a white man's property. And her baby Bennie remains a hostage in Virginia, subject to all the cruelties that she has escaped.

WHAT LOOKS LIKE CRAZY ON AN ORDINARY DAY
Cleage, Pearl
William Morrow, 244 pgs., 1998, $13.00
ISBN 038079487X

As a girl growing up in Idlewild, Michigan, Ava Johnson had always heard that, if you were young, black, and had any sense at all, Atlanta was the place to be. So as soon as she was old enough and able, that was where she went. Now, after more than a decade, Ava has come home. Ava Johnson has tested positive for HIV. And she's back in little Idlewild to spend a quiet summer with her widowed sister Joyce, before moving on to finish her life in San Francisco. But what she thinks is the end is only the beginning because there's too much going down in her hometown for Ava to ignore.

THE WAKE OF THE WIND
Cooper, J. California
Anchor Books, 384 pgs., 1999, $13.95
ISBN 0385487053

Set in the South during the waning years of the Civil War, this is the dramatic story of a remarkable heroine, Lifee, and her husband, Mor. When emancipation finally comes to Texas, Mor, Lifee, and their family set out in search of hope and a piece of land they can work and call their own. Miraculously, they manage not only to survive, but also to succeed. Their crops grow, their children thrive, they educate themselves and others. But the South during Reconstruction is not a place that takes kindly to the achievements of former slaves, and as lynchings and injustice become a plague across the region, time and again they must make the anguished decision to leave their land in search of a safer place.

Krik? Krak!
Danticat, Edwidge
Vintage, 240 pgs., 1996, $12.00
ISBN 067976657X

Nine powerful stories about life under Haiti's dictatorships: the terrorism of the Tonton Macoutes; the slaughtering of hope and the resiliency of love; about those who fled to America to give their children a better life and those who stayed behind in the villages; about the linkages of generations of women through the magical tradition of storytelling.

My Soul to Keep
Due, Tananarive
William Morrow & Company, 352 pgs., 1998, $15.95
ISBN 006105366X

Jessica is a Miami investigative reporter with a beautiful daughter, Kira, and a husband, David, so loving, brilliant, and attentive that she calls him Mr. Perfect. Suddenly, however, her life takes a terrifying turn. Her best friend is brutally and mysteriously murdered and Jessica discovers an ancient, unimaginable danger that will shatter her life and family forever. She learns that her husband is Dawit, an immortal who, more than four hundred years ago, was one of a sect of Ethiopian scholars who traded their souls for eternal life. In *My Soul to Keep*, the worlds of Jessica and Dawit collide with harrowing, unforgettable consequences as Jessica learns firsthand the terrible price for eternal life.

Watershed
Everett, Percival
Beacon Press, 224 pgs., 2003, $14.00
ISBN 0807083615

On a windswept landscape somewhere north of Denver, Colorado, Robert Hawks, a feisty and dangerously curious hydrologist, finds himself enmeshed in a fight over Native American treaty rights. What begins for Robert as a peaceful fishing interlude ends in murder and the disclosure of government secrets.

ERASURE
Everett, Percival
Hyperion, 304 pgs., 2002, $14.95
ISBN 0786888156

Thelonious (Monk) Ellison has never allowed race to define his identity. But as both a writer and an African American, he is offended and angered by the success of *We's Lives in Da Ghetto*. Hailed as an authentic representation of the African American experience, the book is a national best-seller. The book's success rankles all the more as Monk's own most recent novel has just notched its seventh rejection. Then, in a heat of inspiration and energy, Monk composes a fierce parody of the sort of exploitative, ghetto wanna-be literature represented by *We's Lives in Da Ghetto*. The author is greeted as an authentic new voice of black America. Monk—or his pseudonymous alter ego, Stagg R. Leigh—is offered money, fame, success beyond anything Monk has known. And as demand begins to build for meetings with and appearances by Leigh, Monk is faced with a whole new set of problems.

CHILD OF GOD
Files, Lolita
Simon & Schuster, 320 pgs., 2002, $13.00
ISBN 0743225910

Everybody knows everybody else's business in Downtown, Tennessee. Neighbors swap rumors about voodoo, incest and illegitimate children. Usually they're gossiping about the Boten clan. In this epic family saga, Lolita Files unveils the hidden lives of three generations of the Boten family. The family's past begins rising to the surface when a mysterious fire takes the life of young Ophelia Boten's infant son. The tragedy sets the family in motion, its members on a quest for self-discovery that will lead them to the drug world of inner-city Detroit, a midwestern college campus, the jungles of Vietnam and back again.

Divine Days
Forrest, Leon
W.W. Norton, 1,144 pgs., 1994, $18.00
ISBN 0393312216

   Divine Days explores the mythical world of Leon Forrest's literary kingdom, Forest County. It's set in bars, churches and barbershops over a crucial seven-day period in the life of would-be playwright Joubert Jones during February 1966. *Divine Days* creates a profound microcosm of African American life. Joubert Jones, playwright, journalist, bartender and lover, confronts and transcends the power of a fantastic group of bar denizens whose personalities run the gamut of classical myths, Shakespearean heroes, Shakespearean villains, religious true-believers and ghetto dwellers.

Billy
French, Albert L.
Penguin USA, 224 pgs., 1995, $12.95
ISBN 0140179089

   Albert French lights up the monstrous face of American racism in this harrowing tale of ten-year-old Billy Lee Turner, who is convicted of and executed for murdering a white girl in Banes County, Mississippi, in 1937. *Billy* is about the deaths of two children—one girl, one boy—the girl's death an accident, the boy's a murder perpetrated by the state. Though the events *Billy* records occur during the 1930s in a small Mississippi town, the range of characters, emotions and social forces, and the inexorable march to doom of a ten-year-old boy and the society that dooms him, catapult the story far beyond a specific time and location.

A Gathering of Old Men
Gaines, Ernest J.
Vintage, 214 pgs., 1992, $11.00
ISBN 0679738908

   Set on a Louisiana sugarcane plantation in the 1970s, *A Gathering of Old Men* is a powerful depiction of racial tensions arising over the death of a Cajun farmer at the hands of a black man. When the sheriff arrives to investigate the death of Beau Bouton he finds eighteen old black men with recently fired rifles claiming responsibility for the death of Beau. Published in 1983, *A Gathering of Old Men* became a made-for-television movie starring Louis Gossett Jr.

A LESSON BEFORE DYING
Gaines, Ernest J.
Vintage, 256 pgs., 1997, $12.95
ISBN 0375702709

How do you teach a man to die with dignity—especially when he is innocent of the crime for which he has been sentenced to death? *A Lesson Before Dying* explores the themes of manhood, racism, family and community. Jefferson, a twenty-one-year-old black man, is accused of the murder of a white shopkeeper. Jefferson is further victimized when his defense lawyer compares his intelligence to that of an animal. Set in a small Cajun community in the late 1940s, *A Lesson Before Dying* is the story of one man condemned to die and the young teacher who visits him in his cell.

THE NORTON ANTHOLOGY OF AFRICAN AMERICAN LITERATURE
Gates, Henry Louis, Jr., and Nellie Y. McKay, eds.
W.W. Norton, 2,665 pgs., 1997, $63.90 with companion CD
ISBN 0393959082

This landmark anthology includes the work of 120 writers over two centuries, from the earliest known work by an African American, Lucy Terry's poem "Bars Fight," to the fiction of the Nobel Laureate Toni Morrison and the poems of U.S. Poet Laureate Rita Dove.

RHYTHMS
Hill, Donna
Griffin Trade Paperback, 336 pgs., 2002, $12.95
ISBN 0312300697

After the sudden and tragic death of her parents, Cora Harvey has nothing left except her incredible voice and her dream to share it with the world. But her dream will never come true in Rudell, Mississippi, especially if she marries the man she adores, Dr. David Mackey. When she sets out for Chicago, everyone in the small town, including David, believes that the next time they see Cora her name will be in lights. But it's not long before Cora finds herself back in Rudell and back in David's arms harboring a secret she dare not reveal, not even to her husband-to-be.

THE RIVER WHERE BOOLD IS BORN
Jackson-Opoku, Sandra
Ballantine Books, 432 pgs., 1998, $12.95
ISBN 034542476X

The River Where Blood Is Born takes us on a journey along the river of one family's history, carving a course across two centuries and three continents, from ancient Africe into today's America. Here, through the lives of Mother Africa's many daughters, we come to understand the real meaning of roots.

A VISITATION OF SPIRITS
Kenan, Randall
Vintage, 257 pgs., 2000, $13.00
ISBN 0375703977

Sixteen-year-old Horace Cross is plagued by demons that take shape in his mind, culminating in one night of horrible and tragic transformation. In the face of Horace's fate, his cousin Reverend James "Jimmy" Green questions the values of a community that nourishes a boy, places their hopes for salvation on him, only to deny him his destiny. Told in a montage of voices and memories, *A Visitation of Spirits* shows just how richly populated a family's present is with the spirits of the past and the future.

PRAISESONG FOR THE WIDOW
Marshall, Paule
Plume, 256 pgs., 1992, $12.95
ISBN 0452267110

Avey Johnson is a West Indian American widow in her sixties. After her husband dies, Avey goes on a cruise and begins having disturbing dreams. She makes plans to return home to New York right away, but a layover in Grenada brings a stranger into her world. The stranger is returning to his island home in Carriacou. Avey goes with the stranger to his island and reconnects with her Caribbean roots.

SUGAR
McFadden, Bernice L.
Plume, 229 pgs., 2001, $13.00
ISBN 0452282209

In *Sugar*, Bernice L. McFadden tells the story of two women: a modest, churchgoing wife and mother, and the young prostitute she befriends. When Sugar arrives in 1950s Bigelow the women hate her from the minute they lay eyes on her. All they know is they want her gone, out of their town, and away from their men. But Sugar has traveled too far and survived too much to back down now. Deep in her soul, Pearl Taylor knows what it is that Sugar feels, because it happened to her. It was the day her world shut down, the day the devil himself murdered her young daughter Jude. It wasn't that Pearl stopped believing in God, exactly; she just couldn't trust him the way she used to. Then Sugar moves in next door and Pearl's life changes.

TUMBLING
McKinney-Whetstone, Diane
Touchstone, 352 pgs., 1997, $12.00
ISBN 0684837242

Herbie and Noon care deeply for each other but have been unable to consummate their marriage. So, while Noon finds comfort and solace in her church, club-hopping Herbie finds friendship and sexual gratification with a jazz singer named Ethel. Unexpectedly, Herbie and Noon are blessed with daughters when, on two separate occasions, children are left on their doorstep. Set in South Philadelphia during the 1940s and 1950s, when a devastating city proposal threatens to put a road through the area, the community must pull together to avoid being torn apart. Noon becomes the unexpected leader in the struggle to keep both her home and her family whole.

Mama
McMillan, Terry
Pocket Books, 320 pgs., 1995, $7.99
ISBN 0671884484

Mildred Peacock is the funny, feisty heroine of *Mama*, a survivor who'll do anything to keep her family together. In Mildred's world, men come and go as quickly as her paychecks, but her five children are her dream, her hope and her future. This is McMillan's first book, published in 1983.

Breaking Ice: An Anthology of Contemporary African-American Fiction
McMillan, Terry, ed.
Penguin USA, 690 pgs., 1990, $18.00
ISBN 0140116974

Breaking Ice is a striking collection of contemporary authors, both established and emerging, among them are Barbara Neely, Ernest Gaines, Toni Cade Bambara, Percival Everett and J. California Cooper.

Devil in a Blue Dress
Mosley, Walter
Washington Square Press, 272 pgs., 2002, $14.00
ISBN 0743451791

Los Angeles, 1948: Easy Rawlins is a black war veteran just fired from his job at a defense plant. Easy is drinking in a friend's bar, wondering how he'll meet his mortgage, when a white man in a linen suit walks in and offers good money if Easy will simply locate Miss Daphne Money, a blond beauty known to frequent black jazz clubs. *Devil in a Blue Dress* was made into a feature film starring Denzel Washington.

SIX EASY PIECES
Mosley, Walter
Washington Square Press, 288 pgs., 2003, $14.00
ISBN 0743442520

Mouse is back! Raymond "Mouse" Alexander returns in *Six Easy Pieces*. Beginning each book is a never-before-published story bringing the Rawlins saga further through the 1960s as Easy works a steady job as the head custodian of Sojourner Truth High School. Together, the stories—"Smoke," "Crimson Stain," "Silver Lining," "Lavender," "Grey-Eyed Death," "Gator Green" and the never-before-published "Amber Gate"—create a single narrative charting Easy's midlife sorrows and realizations.

DOUGLASS' WOMEN
Rhodes, Jewell Parker
Washington Square Press, 384 pgs., 2003, $14.00
ISBN 0743410092

Douglass' Women reimagines the lives of an American hero, Frederick Douglass, and two women—his wife and his mistress—who loved him and lived in his shadow. Anna Douglass was a free woman of color and Douglass's wife of forty-four years who bore him five children. Ottilie Assing was a German-Jewish intellectual who provided him the companionship of the mind that he needed. Hurt by Douglass's infidelity, Anna rejected his notion that only literacy freed the mind. For her, familial love rivaled intellectual pursuits. Ottilie was raised by parents who embraced the ideal of free love, but found herself for nearly three decades in an unfulfilling love triangle with America's most famous self-taught slave.

THE DRIFT
Ridley, John
Alfred A. Knopf, 288 pgs., 2002, $24.00
ISBN 0375411828

Charles Harmon, a black man "living white" and living well in an upper-upper-middle-class suburb of Los Angeles, becomes Brain Nigger Charlie, a train tramp, leaning on drugs to keep him from thinking about everything he had. Charlie's been asked to find the niece of the man who taught him how to survive the rails—a girl lost somewhere on the High Line, the "corridors of racist hate" along the tracks of the Pacific Northwest. Charlie has little hope of finding her alive. The search is a twisted trail of lies and deceit, hate and hopelessness, and brutal unsolved murders.

THE COLOR PURPLE
Walker, Alice
Washington Square Press, 256 pgs., 1998, $14.00
ISBN 0671019074

The Color Purple is foremost the story of Celie, a poor, barely literate Southern black woman who struggles to escape the brutality and degradation of her treatment by men. The tale is told primarily through letters, which, out of isolation and despair, she initially addresses to God. During the course of the novel, Celie frees herself from her husband's repressive control. Publication of *The Color Purple* established Alice Walker as a major voice in modern fiction. Her unforgettable portrait of Celie and her friends, family and lovers is rich with passion, pain, inspiration and an indomitable love of life. *The Color Purple* was adapted to film in 1985 starring Whoopi Goldberg and Danny Glover.

HARLEM REDUX
Walker, Persia
Simon & Schuster, 320 pgs., 2002, $23.00
ISBN 0743224973

Four years after dropping out of Harlem society, David McKay, a handsome young lawyer from a prominent Strivers' Row family, returns home, devastated by the news of his sister Lillian's suicide. Burdened by a secret of his own, David stays in Harlem just long enough to stave off the threat to his family home and answer questions about Lillian's death. Yet the deeper he probes, the closer he comes to unleashing forces that threaten to reveal his own crippling secret—a secret that could either destroy or redeem him.

THE DEVIL RIDING (A TAMARA HAYLE MYSTERY)
Wesley, Valerie Wilson
Avon, 304 pgs., 2002, $6.99
ISBN 0380732084

Darnella Desmond, stepdaughter to wealthy Foster Desmond, leaves her plush home for the wilds of Atlantic City, eschewing all contact with her family. When Darnella's last-known roommate is murdered, apparently by a serial killer stalking Atlantic City's vulnerable runaway population, Darnella's mother hires Tamara Hayle to track her daughter down. As her investigation brings her closer to Darnella, Tamara discovers that at the heart of the young woman's disappearance lie two generations' worth of familial perversity—and a legacy of betrayal that threatens to undo the Desmond family.

THE WEDDING
West, Dorothy
Anchor Books, 240 pgs., 1996, $12.00
ISBN 0385471440

Written in 1995 by the last remaining member of the Harlem Renaissance writers, *The Wedding* centers around the Oval, a very special community on the island of Martha's Vineyard. An enclave for the black middle class, the Oval has flourished since the turn of the century, but it will never be the same as one of its daughters, Shelby Coles, prepares to marry a white jazz musician, a decision that threatens to tear her family apart. Enter Lute McNeil, a social-climbing Boston businessman who sees in Shelby and her family everything he could ever want for his three motherless daughters. Lute begins his pursuit of Shelby with disastrous results.

THE INTUITIONIST
Whitehead, Colson
Anchor Books, 256 pgs., 2000, $12.95
ISBN 0385493002

It is a time of calamity in a major metropolitan city's Department of Elevator Inspectors, and Lila Mae Watson, the first black female elevator inspector in the history of the department, is at the center of it. Lila Mae is an intuitionist and, it just so happens, has the highest accuracy rate in the entire department. But when an elevator in a new city building goes into total free fall on Lila Mae's watch, chaos ensues.

JOHN HENRY DAYS
Whitehead, Colson
Anchor Books, 400 pgs., 2002, $14.00
ISBN 0385498209

In *John Henry Days*, the narrative revolves around the story of J. Sutter, a young black journalist. Sutter is a "junketeer," a freeloading hack who roams from one publicity event to another, abusing his expense account and mooching as much as possible. An assignment for a travel website takes Sutter to West Virginia for the first annual "John Henry Days" festival, a celebration of a new U.S. postage stamp honoring John Henry. And there the real story of John Henry emerges.

THE HOMEWOOD TRILOGY
Wideman, John Edgar
University of Pittsburgh Press, 536 pgs., 1992, $24.95
ISBN 0822938316

The Homewood Trilogy is comprised of three books describing the black middle-class Pittsburgh community of Homewood, founded by a runaway slave. The other two books are *Hiding Place* (1981) and *Sent for You Yesterday* (1983).

HEALTH

African Americans are disproportionately affected with health problems, from high blood pressure, asthma and diabetes to lupus and sickle-cell anemia. Addictions to drugs and dangerous lifestyles (violence and aggression) are also some of the leading causes of death in the African American community.

Our diet and lifestyle (too often sedentary) contribute greatly to chronic health conditions. Every African American library should have information regarding the major health issues that affect African Americans. The more you understand about health and illness, the better you will be able to take care of yourself and your family.

THE AFRICAN AMERICAN HEALTHBOOK: A PRESCRIPTION FOR IMPROVEMENT
Alcena, Valiere
Citadel Press, 274 pgs., 1996, $12.95
ISBN 0806517190

The African American Healthbook covers almost every health problem that afflicts Americans in general and the black population in particular. Special attention is given to cancer, heart ailments, hypertension, emphysema, diabetes, sickle-cell anemia and drug and alcohol abuse.

BACK TO EDEN
Kloss, Jethro
Lotus Press, 936 pgs., 1990, $9.95
ISBN 0940985101

Jethro Kloss, one of the early pioneers in herbal remedies, found that nature works better than drugs in his crusade for better health. *Back to Eden* has changed many people's lives since its original publication in 1939.

NATURAL HEALTH FOR AFRICAN AMERICANS:
THE PHYSICIANS' GUIDE

Walker, Marcellus A., M.D., and Kenneth B. Singleton, M.D.
Warner Books, 368 pgs., 1999, $14.00
ISBN 0446673692

Natural Health for African Americans: The Physicians' Guide is a resource and guide to taking control of your health. The authors include factors that must be considered when taking a holistic approach to healing. These factors are psychological conditions, such as anxiety, depression and stress; spiritual factors, such as faith and personal integrity; and physical factors such as lifestyle, nutrition and exercise.

CULTURE
AND ANTHROPOLOGY

Anthropology is the study of people and their cultures, which is important for African Americans because of the blanks that need to be filled in our history. We are an amalgam of cultures and heritages. The influence on American culture began when the first Africans set foot on these shores. Yet many of the cultural influences are so ingrained in American culture that the origins are lost, forgotten or overlooked.

The influence of African and other cultural traditions makes African Americans a unique community. Many are descendants of those who were brought to American shores in chains, while others are descendants of those who voluntarily immigrated to America. We share ancestry with Native American and Caribbean peoples; some even have ancestral ties to Asia, South America and Europe.

These books will open doors to new insights on the African American experience. Hopefully they will shed some light on the contributions African Americans have made to American society.

BLACK RICE: THE AFRICAN ORIGINS OF RICE CULTIVATION IN THE AMERICAS
Carney, Judith A.
Harvard University Press, 256 pgs., 2001, $15.95
ISBN 0674008340

Few Americans identify slavery with the cultivation of rice. Yet rice was a major plantation crop during the first three centuries of settlement in the Americas. Rice accompanied African slaves across the Middle Passage throughout the New World to Brazil, the Caribbean and the southern United States. By the middle of the eighteenth century, rice plantations in South Carolina and the black slaves who worked them had created one of the most profitable economies in the world.

A COMMUNION OF SPIRITS: AFRICAN AMERICAN QUILTERS, PRESERVERS, AND THEIR STORIES
Freeman, Roland
Rutledge Hill Press, 396 pgs., 1996, $34.95
ISBN 1558534253

The first national survey of African American quiltmakers, this beautiful book presents the quilters the author met across

America over a twenty-year period. Their stories and quilts both inform and inspire.

The Legacy of Ibo Landing: Gullah Roots of African American Culture
Goodwine, Marquetta, et al.
Clarity Press, 208 pgs., 1998, $27.95
ISBN 0932863256

Marquetta Goodwine is a member of two families that have a long history in the Sea Islands. *The Legacy of Ibo Landing* begins with the story of Ibo (Igbo) warriors who refused to be enslaved, who, with their chains, walked into the waters of the Georgia coast. Some say they walked back to Africa. Descendants of formerly enslaved Africans, many of whom fled their enslavement, now known as Gullah people, number some 500,000 strong and still speak the Gullah language. They now fight to keep their homes and land from the hands of developers who would bring an end to their way of life.

Breaking Ground, Breaking Silence: The Story of New York's African Burial Ground
Hansen, Joyce
Henry Holt, 130 pgs., 1997, $17.95
ISBN 0805050124

Although this book was written for children, it is very much appreciated by people of all ages. It's an important book that chronicles one of the most astonishing events of the twentieth century for African Americans. In 1991 an African burial ground was discovered in lower Manhattan—the final resting place of over twenty thousand enslaved and free Africans buried there in the eighteenth century. The dig uncovered four hundred graves with skeletal remains and artifacts, enabling anthropologists and archaeologists to learn a great deal about the Africans and their culture and lifestyle in old New York during the Colonial period. Many of the Africans died within two years after arriving in New York and others were literally worked to death as evidenced by trauma or injuries to their bones, especially neck bones.

BLACK GODS: ORISA STUDIES IN THE NEW WORLD
Mason, John
Yoruba Theological Seminary, 100 pgs., 1998, $10.00
ISBN 1881244083

Thirteen major Yoruba deities are discussed in depth. Their symbols, personal characteristics, philosophical values, animal familiars, corresponding body parts and feast days are all reviewed.

THE GULLAH PEOPLE AND THEIR AFRICAN HERITAGE
Pollitzer, William S.
University of Georgia Press, 336 pgs., 1999, $40.00

Anthropologist William S. Pollitzer discusses aspects of Gullah history and culture—language, religion, family and social relationships, music, folklore, trades and skills, and arts and crafts. Readers will learn of the indigo-and-rice-growing skills that slaves taught to their masters, the echoes of an African past that are woven into baskets and stitched into quilts, the form and phrasing that identify Gullah speech and much more.

THE BLACK SEMINOLES: HISTORY OF A FREEDOM-SEEKING PEOPLE
Porter, Kenneth
University Press of Florida, 352 pgs., 1996, $29.95
ISBN 0813014514

This story of a remarkable people, the Black Seminoles, and their charismatic leader, Chief John Horse, chronicles their heroic struggle for freedom. Beginning in the early 1800s, small groups of fugitive slaves living in Florida joined the Seminole Indians—an association that thrived for decades on reciprocal respect and affection.

MAROON SOCIETIES: REBEL SLAVE COMMUNITIES IN THE AMERICAS
Price, Richard, ed.
Johns Hopkins University Press, 445 pgs., 1996, $19.95
ISBN 0801854962

Maroon Societies offers a systematic study of the communities formed by escaped slaves in the Caribbean, Latin America and the United States. The volume includes eyewitness accounts written by escaped slaves and their pursuers, as well as modern historical and anthropological studies of the maroon experience. For this edition, Richard Price has written a new preface reflecting recent changes in both maroon scholarship and in the lives of contemporary maroons throughout the Americas.

Spoken Soul: The Story of Black English

Rickford, John Russell, and Russell John Rickford
John Wiley & Sons, 288 pgs., 2000, $15.95
ISBN 0471399574

Linguist John Rickford provides the definitive guide to black English from its origins, to its new directions, to its powerful fascination for society at large. *Spoken Soul* is loaded with examples from such icons as August Wilson, Richard Pryor and Eddie Murphy. Rickford also crashes through the rigid divisions separating "high" and "low" culture. Telling the story of the language links such apparently disparate figures as Toni Morrison, Jesse Jackson and Lauryn Hill.

The Divine Nine: The History of African American Fraternities and Sororities

Ross, Lawrence C., Jr.
Dafina Books, 465 pgs., 2001, $16.00
ISBN 0758202709

America's black fraternities and sororities are a unique and vital part of twentieth-century African American history. Since the creation of the first fraternity in 1906 at Cornell University, they have provided young black achievers with opportunities to support one another while serving their communities and the nation. *The Divine Nine* tells the story of how these organizations have played a major role in shaping generations of black leaders.

THE WAYS OF BLACK FOLK: A YEAR IN THE LIFE OF A PEOPLE

Ross, Lawrence C., Jr.
Dafina Books, 400 pgs., 2003, $24.00
ISBN 0758200579

Ross profiles men and women from diverse walks of life, economic backgrounds and cultures who still have one thing in common. Here, such figures as *New York Times* best-selling author E. Lynn Harris, poet Nikki Giovanni, Dave Matthews Band musician Boyd Tinsley and member of the British Parliament David Lammy are filed side by side with everyday brothers and sisters living through similar challenges and triumphs.

HIDDEN IN PLAIN VIEW: A SECRET STORY OF QUILTS AND THE UNDERGROUND RAILROAD

Tobin, Jacqueline
Doubleday, 240 pgs., 2000, $14.00
ISBN 0385497679

Hidden in Plain View tells the fascinating story of a friendship, a lost tradition and an incredible discovery, explaining for the first time how enslaved men and women encoded messages within quilt patterns that helped fugitives navigate their escape along the Underground Railroad.

CERAMIC UNCLES AND CELLULOID MAMMIES: BLACK IMAGES AND THEIR INFLUENCE ON CULTURE

Turner, Patricia A.
University of Virginia Press, 238 pgs., 2002, $16.50
ISBN 0813921554

Patricia Turner investigates the way black culture has been distorted and used throughout American history, from Aunt Jemima cookie jars, Darkie toothpaste, to the Disney film *Roger Rabbit*. Turner also investigates the ways blacks have responded and countered such distortions.

STYLIN': AFRICAN AMERICAN EXPRESSIVE CULTURE, FROM ITS BEGINNINGS TO THE ZOOT SUIT
White, Shane, and Graham White
Cornell University Press, 320 pgs., 1999, $17.95
ISBN 0801482836

Shane White and Graham White consider the deeper significance of the ways in which African Americans have dressed, walked, danced, arranged their hair and communicated in silent gestures. They ask what elaborate hairstyles, bright colors, bandannas, long watch chains and zoot suits, for example, have really meant, and discuss style itself as an expression of deep-seated cultural imperatives.

AFRICAN AMERICAN HOLIDAYS
Winchester, Faith
Bridgestone Books, 24 pgs., 1999, $18.60
ISBN 1560654562

Although written for children, this book holds information that will delight adults as well. Winchester discusses special times of the year when African Americans celebrate Black History Month, Mardi Gras, Juneteenth, Harambee, Junkanoo and Kwanzaa.

MUSIC

African Americans have had a profound effect on the evolution and development of music in America and in the African diaspora. Bringing their musical traditions with them to the New World, the African influence on American music began on the slave ships where the captives were forced to sing and dance for exercise. Later, on plantations, they were forbidden to practice their religions, which included the drum as a sacred object—it was feared that the slaves would use the drum to communicate with one another. Instead, they continued to raise their voices in song and use their bodies to accompany their music.

The African slaves, forced into Christianity, retained their African sensibilities, and their musical traditions began to emerge in the late-eighteenth century as they began to sing "spirituals and gospels" in both religious and nonreligious settings—in the fields (work songs) and during after-service gatherings in "praise houses." The call-and-response, hand and thigh clapping, foot stomping and shouting (hollers) of African tradition were incorporated into the spiritual expression.

Later, African American musical traditions evolved into the blues, ragtime, Dixieland, jazz, boogie, swing and bebop. These were followed by rock 'n' roll, soul, rhythm and blues, rap and hip-hop—all of which have had a profound influence on music all over the world. The African roots have found their way back home dressed in New World clothing.

TEMPLES OF SOUND: INSIDE THE GREAT RECORDING STUDIOS
Cogan, Jim, and William Clark
Chronicle Books, 224 pgs., 2003, $24.95
ISBN 0811833941

All great music has a birthplace. *Temples of Sound* tells the stories of the legendary studios where musical genius and a magical space came together to capture some of the most exciting jazz, pop, funk, soul and country records ever made. From the celebrated southern studios of Sun and Stax, to the John Coltrane/Miles Davis sessions in producer Rudy Van Gelder's living room, each of the fifteen profiles in this book brings great music to life at the moment of its creation.

JAZZ: THE ESSENTIAL COMPANION FOR EVERY JAZZ FAN
Fordham, John
Dorling Kindersley, 216 pgs., 1999, $29.95
ISBN 0760715661

Jazz traces the origins of jazz from Africa and the South to contemporary times, and looks at the future of this musical art form. Fordham uses time lines that show chronologically the major persons, places and events of jazz history. He provides profiles of twenty major jazz artists from ragtime to Dixieland, bebop, cool jazz, free jazz, fusion and more. In his section on instruments and techniques, Fordham shows the craftsmanship of instruments, accompanied by jazz techniques demonstrated by contemporary artists. The section on classic recordings is very impressive because it lists African musicians, like Salif Keita and Dollar Brand, as well as American artists.

Hip Hop America
George, Nelson
Penguin USA, 224 pgs., 1999, $13.95
ISBN 0140280227

Hip Hop America is the history of hip-hop from its roots in the late 1970s to its emergence as the cultural force that today influences everything from movies to fashion, advertising to sports. It's the story of a society-altering collision between black youth culture and the mass media—and it's very big business. Examining hip-hop as music, a style, a business, a myth and a moral code, Nelson George turns hip-hop over to look at the ways it has been treated by Hollywood, Madison Avenue and Wall Street to reach not just young black consumers but all young people. *Hip Hop America* shows us why, against all odds, hip-hop has held a steady grip on American popular culture for over twenty years.

Standing in the Shadow of Motown: The Life and Music of Legendary Bassist James Jamerson
Licks, Dr., ed.
Hal Leonard Publishing, 208 pgs., 1991, $35.00 with companion CD
ISBN 0881888826

Bassist James Jamerson was the embodiment of the Motown spirit and groove, the invisible entity whose playing inspired thousands. His tumultuous life and musical brilliance are explored in depth through hundreds of interviews, forty-nine transcribed musical scores, two hours of recorded all-star performances and more than fifty rarely seen photos in this stellar tribute to behind-the-scenes Motown. Features a 120-minute CD.

THE VIBE HISTORY OF HIP HOP
Light, Alan, ed.
Three Rivers Press, 432 pgs., 1999, $27.50
ISBN 0609805037

VIBE, the voice of the hip-hop generation, presents the essence of hip-hop. Music, fashion, dance, graffiti, movies, videos and business—it's all in this tale of a cultural revolution that transcends race and gender, language and nationality. *The VIBE History of Hip Hop* tells the full story of this grassroots cultural movement, from its origins on the streets of the Bronx to its explosion as an international phenomenon. Illustrated with almost two hundred photos, and accompanied by comprehensive discographies, this book is a vivid review of the hip-hop world through the eyes and ears of more than fifty of the finest music writers and cultural critics at work today.

HEART AND SOUL: A CELEBRATION OF BLACK MUSIC STYLE IN AMERICA 1930–1975
Merlis, Bob, et al.
Watson-Guptill Publishers, 160 pgs., 2001, $24.95
ISBN 0823083144

From the decline of the Big Band sound to the emergence of Black Pride, Sly, Superfly and the Funk, *Heart and Soul* celebrates the nearly half-century of the vibrant, flamboyant and extravagant flowering in African American culture that enriched the entire world. The story is filled with characters such as O. V. Wright, a singer deemed "too ugly to tour"; Frankie Lymon, who received a hot dog as full payment for some of the greatest R&B songs of all time; Billie Holiday shooting dice with the boys on the bus; Solomon Burke; Screamin' Jay Hawkins who was locked in his coffin by the Drifters; and many other talented and unique entertainers.

Go Down Moses: Celebrating the African-American Spiritual
Newman, Richard, ed.
Clarkson Potter, 224 pgs., 1998, $30.00
ISBN 0609600311

"Go Down Moses" was the first African American spiritual to be written down. The enslaved African Americans saw themselves in the stories of the Israelites and likened the South to Pharaoh's Egypt. They looked for liberation and a leader. But the songs in this anthology are not just spirituals; they are also messages from our ancestors. They were sung as freedom songs, hidden messages and songs with double meanings. This is an easy-to-read anthology of over two hundred songs. Newman provides music for some of the most commonly known and popular songs.

Dancing in the Street: Motown and the Cultural Politics of Detroit
Smith, Suzanne E.
Harvard University Press, 336 pgs., 2001, $15.95
ISBN 0674005465

Detroit in the 1960s was a city with a pulse; people were marching in step with Martin Luther King Jr., dancing in the street with Martha and the Vandellas and facing off with city police. Through it all, Motown provided the beat. This book tells the story of Motown—as both musical style and entrepreneurial phenomenon—and of its intrinsic relationship to the politics and culture of Motor Town, USA.

The Music of Black Americans: A History
Southern, Eileen
W.W. Norton, 640 pgs., 1997, $41.75
ISBN 0393038432

Beginning with the arrival of the first Africans in the English colonies, Eileen Southern weaves a fascinating narrative of intense musical activity that has not only played a vital role in the lives of black Americans, but has also deeply influenced music performances in the United States and around the world. Southern fully chronicles the singers, instrumentalists and composers who created this rich body of music and skillfully describes the genres and styles that characterize it from its earliest manifestations among a people in slavery, to the rap beat of the late-twentieth century.

AND SO I SING: AFRICAN AMERICAN DIVAS OF OPERA AND CONCERT
Story, Rosalyn
Amistad, 272 pgs., 1993, $12.95
ISBN 1567430112

Black women bring a host of influences and ideologies with them to opera—as well as their spirituality, their strengths and their passions. The exclusion of blacks from opera for so many generations impoverished both the artists and the artistic world from which they were barred. This book not only supplies portraits of the greatest artists for future generations of students of black art and culture, but also rescues from history's shadows the lost legacies of geniuses born too soon.

AFRICAN AMERICAN MUSICIANS
Tate, Eleanora E., edited by Jim Haskins
John Wiley & Sons, 170 pgs., 2000, $22.95
ISBN 0471253561

This collection of profiles tells the inspiring stories of twenty-five African American musicians: both the legendary and the forgotten musical heroes whose contributions to the industry were invaluable to those who followed in their footsteps. Each biography—including many music industry giants, as well as lesser-known names—covers a musician's origins, challenges and accomplishments. Although written for children, this book is a valuable addition to the family library.

FUNK: THE MUSIC, THE PEOPLE, AND THE RHYTHM OF THE ONE
Vincent, Rickey
St. Martin's Press, 375 pgs., 1996, $15.95
ISBN 0312134991

Rickey Vincent's *Funk* celebrates the songs, the musicians, the philosophy and the meaning of funk. The book spans from the early work of James Brown through today. *Funk* tells the history of a uniquely American form of music born out of tradition and community, filled with energy, attitude, anger, hope and an irrepressible spirit.

Jazz: A History of America's Music
Ward, Geoffrey C., and Ken Burns
Alfred A. Knopf, 512 pgs., 2002, $29.95
ISBN 0679765395

This is the companion book to the nineteen-hour PBS television series. Filmmakers Ken Burns and Geoffrey Ward bring us the history of the first American music. In words and photographs—some never before published—we meet Louis Armstrong, Bessie Smith, Duke Ellington, Billie Holiday, Benny Goodman, Ella Fitzgerald, Charlie Parker, Miles Davis, John Coltrane, Dizzy Gillespie, Dave Brubeck and many more. Contributors Wynton Marsalis, Dan Morgenstern, Gerald Early, Stanley Crouch and Gary Giddins put the evolution of jazz in cultural context.

Ev'ry Time I Feel the Spirit: 101 Best-Loved Psalms, Gospel Hymns and Spiritual Songs of the African-American Church
Warren, Gwendolin Sims
Owl Books, 372 pgs., 1999, $15.00
ISBN 0805044116

Complete with sheet music throughout, this volume profiles 101 of the best-loved psalms, gospel hymns and spiritual songs of the African American church.

Jùjú: A Social History and Ethnography of an African Popular Music
Waterman, Christopher Alan
University of Chicago Press, 278 pgs., 1990, $21.00
ISBN 0226874656

Most African Americans have never heard of Captain Jide

Ojo, King Sunny Ade, Fela Kuti, Chief Commander Ebenezer Obey or Tunde King. But it's important to recognize the contributions of Nigerian musicians to the ever-growing genre of world music. African Americans, for the most part, have ancestral ties to West Africa. For us, jùjú is "roots" music. Waterman includes photographs of the great jùjú musicians and also provides a glimpse into Yoruban society. Photographs of the dance clubs and hotels give an insider's look at the entertainment world of Nigeria. There is also a ninety-minute cassette tape with examples of the music to accompany the text, available for order.

ART

In the nineteenth century, African American artists followed the traditions of European or English classic styles. Self-expression was not a luxury afforded to African American artists. Color was the determining factor in who could attend schools and colleges for the arts. African American artisans were woodworkers, sculptors, painters, potters, silversmiths and much more.

Many African American artists worked only for the sake of their art and did not receive compensation, frequently creating works of art for their master's household, and sometimes for other white people. Some of the lucky ones were able to buy their freedom by bartering their skills.

After the Civil War, African American artists began to find recognition for their work—even being exhibited in museums—but they still had to follow the classic and European models. Because of this, many artists went to Europe, where they were free to find their own expression.

The books in this section feature artists such as Horace Woodroff, Meta Warwick Fuller, Henry Ossawa Tanner, Jacob Lawrence and Romare Bearden, who paved the way for artists such as Keith Piper and Renée Cox.

HARLEM RENAISSANCE: ART OF BLACK AMERICA
Driskell, David C., et al.
Abradale Press, 200 pgs., 1994, $39.95
ISBN 0810981289

This book focuses on the fine artists who achieved international fame during the Harlem Renaissance: sculptor Meta Warwick Fuller, painter and illustrator Aaron Douglas and painters Palmer Hayden and William H. Johnson. Complementing their art are the photographs of James Van Der Zee, the great documentary photographer who captured images of Harlem and its citizens, from celebrities and major social occasions to ordinary families, store fronts and street scenes.

AFRICAN AMERICAN ART: ART AND ARTIST
Lewis, Samella
University of California Press, 359 pgs., 2003, $29.95
ISBN 0520239350

African American Art looks at the works and lives of artists from the eighteenth century to the present, including new work in traditional media as well as in installation art, mixed media and digital/computer art. This book presents the rich legacy of work done by African American artists who are now included in the permanent collections of national and international museums, as well as in major private collections.

AFRICAN-AMERICAN ARTISTS, 1929–1945: PRINTS, DRAWINGS, AND PAINTINGS IN THE METROPOLITAN MUSEUM OF ART

Messinger, Lisa Mintz, and Lisa Gail Collins, eds.
Yale University Press, 96 pgs., 2003, $14.95
ISBN 0300098774

This book focuses on the work of African American artists during the Depression and the war years, 1929–1945. The catalog features the work of Robert Blackburn, Raymond Steth, Horace Woodroff and Dox Trash, among others, with a smaller selection of paintings and watercolors by such notable artists as Horace Pippin, Romare Bearden, Jacob Lawrence and Bill Traylor. Most of the works in this volume are recent acquisitions of the Metropolitan Museum of Art and have not been previously published.

BLACK ART: A CULTURAL HISTORY (WORLD OF ART SERIES)

Powell, Richard J.
Thames & Hudson, 272 pgs., 2003, $16.95
ISBN 0500203628

The African diaspora—a direct result of the transatlantic slave trade and Western colonialism—generated a wide array of artistic achievements in the past century, from blues to reggae, from the paintings of Henry Ossawa Tanner to the video installations of Keith Piper, as well as artists who have risen to prominence in the past five years, such as Chris Ofili, Kara Walker and Renée Cox. Richard Powell's study concentrates on the works of art themselves and on how these works, created during a time of major social upheaval and transformation, use black culture as both subject and context. Biographies of more than 170 key artists provide a unique art-historical reference.

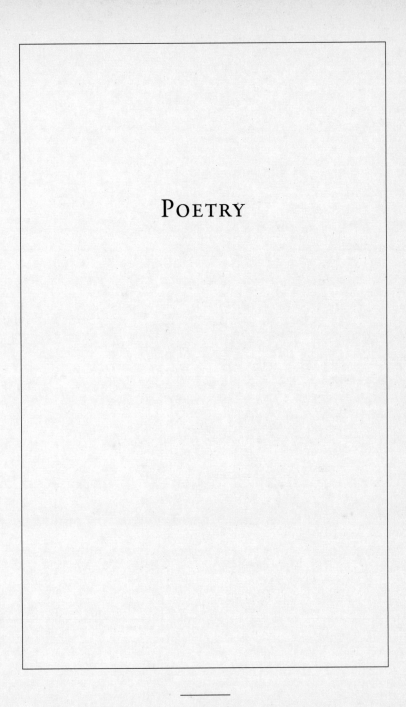

POETRY

$\mathcal{B}$ecause poetry is so personal and subjective, I have not included many books on individual poets. What may be music to my ears may be noise to yours. This has been a difficult section to research. There is an abundance of books of poetry and of the poets themselves. Unfortunately, many are out of print or have limited availability.

What I hope to accomplish in this section is to inspire you to look beyond the listings here and discover for yourself this literary art form. The books I have chosen are mainly anthologies, which offer a sample of poetry from the postslavery era of Phillis Wheatley to the contemporary stylings of Yusef Komunyakaa and everyone in between. I hope you will explore the world of poetry beyond these books.

I Am the Darker Brother: An Anthology of Modern Poems by African Americans
Adoff, Arnold, ed.
Simon & Schuster, 192 pgs., 1996, $4.99
ISBN 0689808690

First published in 1968, this anthology was one of the first collections of African American poetry specifically created with the young reader in mind. Along with selections from Langston Hughes and Gwendolyn Brooks, this newly updated version features poems by such contemporary poets as Maya Angelou, Ishmael Reed, Rita Dove and others.

The Complete Collected Poems of Maya Angelou
Angelou, Maya
Random House, 288 pgs., 1994, $24.00
ISBN 067942895X

This volume comprises five poetry collections by the former poet laureate: *Just Give Me a Cool Drink of Water 'fore I Diiie* (1971); *Oh Pray My Wings Are Gonna Fit Me Well* (1975); *And Still I Rise* (1978); *Shaker, Why Don't You Sing?* (1983); *I Shall Not Be Moved* (1990); and the 1993 inaugural poem "On the Pulse of Morning."

American Negro Poetry: An Anthology
Bontemps, Arna Wendell
Hill and Wang, 256 pgs., 1996, $13.00
ISBN 0809015641

This anthology has for decades been seen as a fundamental collection of African American verse. Bontemps, an important figure during and after the Harlem Renaissance, the author of more than twenty-five novels, and longtime librarian at Fisk University, revised this classic anthology just before his death, adding such crucial new voices as Audre Lorde, Nikki Giovanni and Bob Kaufman, among others.

Selected Poems
Brooks, Gwendolyn
Perennial, 160 pgs., 1999, $12.00
ISBN 0060931744

The classic volume by the distinguished modern poet brings together the best work from three earlier books now out of print, and includes poems not previously published in book form. *Selected Poems* represents her technical mastery, her compassionate and illuminating response to a world that is both special and universal and her warm humanity.

Selected Poems
Dove, Rita
Vintage, 240 pgs., 1993, $13.00
ISBN 0679750800

Here, for the first time in one volume, is a selection of the astonishing poems of Rita Dove, U.S. Poet Laureate 1993–1995, the youngest poet so named and the first African American ever chosen. *Selected Poems* is a collection of Dove's *The Yellow House on the Corner*, which includes a group of poems devoted to the themes of slavery and freedom; *Museum*, intimate ruminations on home and the world; and *Thomas and Beulah*, a verse cycle loosely based on her grandparents' lives.

COLLECTED POETRY OF PAUL LAURENCE DUNBAR

Dunbar, Paul Laurence, edited by Joanne M. Braxton
University of Virginia Press, 344 pgs., 1993, $18.95
ISBN 0813914388

This new edition of the collected poems of Paul Laurence Dunbar, the virtual father of black American poetry, includes sixty poems not included in the previous edition. Sixteen of these poems were found in manuscript form.

THE FURIOUS FLOWERING OF AFRICAN AMERICAN POETRY

Gabbin, Joanne V., ed.
University of Virginia Press, 400 pgs., 1999, $19.50
ISBN 0813918413

This collection of essays and six lively interviews with practicing poets arose from the now-famous Furious Flower Conference of 1994.

CATCH THE FIRE!!!: A CROSS-GENERATIONAL ANTHOLOGY OF CONTEMPORARY AFRICAN-AMERICAN POETRY

Gilbert, Derrick I. M., ed.
Berkley Publishing Group, 320 pgs., 1998, $13.00
ISBN 1573226548

Through the themes of family, the city, revolution, the body and the soul, June Jordan, Amiri Baraka, Abiodun Oyewole (of the Last Poets), Ntozake Shange and Sonia Sanchez discuss their own generation of poets and their thoughts about the emerging poets whose poems they are presenting here.

THE SELECTED POEMS OF NIKKI GIOVANNI (1968–1995)

Giovanni, Nikki
William Morrow, 292 pgs., 1996, $22.00
ISBN 0688140475

When Nikki Giovanni's poems first emerged from the black rights movement in the late 1960s, she immediately took a place among the most celebrated and controversial poets of the era. This is the first compilation of Nikki Giovanni's poetry. It is the testimony of a life's work from one of the most commanding voices to grace America's political and poetic landscape at the end of the twentieth century.

THE COLLECTED POEMS OF STERLING A. BROWN
Harper, Michael S., ed.
Triquarterly, 267 pgs., 1996, $21.00
ISBN 081015045X

Sterling A. Brown was one of the greatest African American poets of the last century, and one of the most important American poets. Brown was a contemporary of Langston Hughes, Claude McKay and Jean Toomer; as a part of this group, and individually, he was instrumental in bringing the traditions of African American folklife to readers all over the world.

THE VINTAGE BOOK OF AFRICAN AMERICAN POETRY
Harper, Michael S., and Anthony Walton, eds.
Vintage, 448 pgs., 2000, $14.00
ISBN 0375703004

Editors Michael S. Harper and Anthony Walton present a collection of black verse in the United States—two hundred years of vision, struggle, power, beauty and triumph from fifty-two outstanding poets.

THE BOOK OF AMERICAN NEGRO POETRY
Johnson, James Weldon
Harcourt, 289 pgs., 1989, $14.00
ISBN 0156135396

In this anthology, James Weldon Johnson gathered not only the best of the Harlem Renaissance writers but also the post–World War I poets such as Countee Cullen and Langston Hughes, who went on to challenge racial stereotypes in an effort to be recognized simply as poets.

THE COLLECTED POEMS OF AUDRE LORDE
Lorde, Audre
W.W. Norton, 512 pgs., 2000, $17.95
ISBN 0393319725

Collected here for the first time are more than three hundred poems from one of this country's major and most influential poets, representing the complete oeuvre of Audre Lorde's poetry. Lorde published nine volumes of poetry which, in her words, detail "a linguistic and emotional tour through the conflicts, fears, and hopes of the world I have inhabited." Included here are Lorde's early, previously unavailable works: "The First Cities," "The New York Head Shop and Museum," "Cables to Rage" and "From a Land Where Other People Live."

THE COLLECTED POEMS OF LANGSTON HUGHES
Rampersad, Arnold, and David Roessel, eds.
Vintage, 736 pgs., 1995, $18.00
ISBN 0679764089

Spanning five decades and comprising 868 poems (nearly 300 of which have never appeared in book form), this volume is the definitive sampling of a writer who has been called the poet laureate of African America—and perhaps our greatest popular poet since Walt Whitman. Here, for the first time, are all the poems that Langston Hughes published during his lifetime, arranged in the general order in which he wrote them and annotated by Arnold Rampersad and David Roessel.

TROUBLE THE WATER: 250 YEARS OF AFRICAN-AMERICAN POETRY
Ward, Jerry W., Jr., ed.
Penguin USA, 592 pgs., 1997, $7.99
ISBN 0451628640

This anthology features over four hundred poems by one hundred of the finest African American poets from the 1700s through the 1990s. Representing 250 years of the black experience, from the moving and powerful oral histories passed on by slaves to the emotional and insightful modern works of Langston Hughes, Alice Walker, Rita Dove, Colleen McElroy and others.

HAIKU: THIS OTHER WORLD
Wright, Richard, edited by Yoshinobu Hakutani
Anchor Books, 320 pgs., 2000, $13.00
ISBN 0385720246

During the last eighteen months of his life, Richard Wright discovered and became enamored of haiku, the strict seventeen-syllable Japanese form. Wright became so excited about the discovery that he began writing his own haiku, eventually writing over four thousand. This book contains the 817 haiku verses he chose for publication before his death.

THE PERFORMING ARTS

African Americans in the arts today owe a great debt to the many performers who paved the way for their acceptance and success in the world of arts and entertainment. It is because of the segregation and rejection of black performers by mainstream America that blacks came together to form all-black dance and theater troupes, to collaborate musically and to create and support their own endeavors.

Prior to 1895, America's black performers were white performers who donned black face paint. Their portrayals of African Americans were offensive and unrealistic and served to reinforce negative stereotypes of shiftless, lazy and childlike Negroes. Blacks desired to see themselves and to be appreciated for their artistic gifts.

Dramatic plays were written in the mid-nineteenth century; Katherine Dunham studied African dance in 1936; Josephine Baker took Paris by storm in 1925; Harry Swan founded the first black-owned record label to record black concert performers in 1921—the list goes on and on. African Americans have had an enormous impact on American culture and these books are just the beginning of unraveling the history of black performance in America.

DANCE

From the slave ships where they were forced to dance for exercise, dance helped captive Africans stay connected to their cultural traditions. Dance is a vital part of African life, celebrating birth, marriage, death and everything in between. With the diversity of African groups came a mixing and melding of different dance traditions forming a new dance aesthetic in the New World.

Black dance moved from the plantations to the minstrel shows of the 1800s, where African Americans performed dances such as the calenda, *the* chica *and the* juba. *In the early 1900s, African dance traditions began to incorporate European traditions such as the Irish jig and clog dancing to create a new form called "tap."*

In the 1930s and 1940s, African Americans began to perform ballet and modern dance. There was also a movement toward African- and Caribbean-influenced dance traditions. Katherine Dunham and Pearl Primus were the foremothers of this dance movement. Over the years, many dancers and choreographers from the late Alvin Ailey and Debbie Allen to Garth Fagan and Bill T. Jones have made enormous contributions to the world of black dance.

Josephine: The Hungry Heart
Baker, Jean-Claude
Cooper Square Press, 592 pgs., 2001, $21.95
ISBN 0815411723

Based on twenty years of research and thousands of interviews, this authoritative biography of performer Josephine Baker, written by her son, provides a candid look at her tempestuous life. Born into poverty in St. Louis, the uninhibited chorus girl became the sensation of Europe and the last century's first black sex symbol. A heroine of the French Resistance in World War II, she entranced figures as diverse as de Gaulle, Tito, Castro, Princess Grace, two popes and Martin Luther King Jr.

Island Possessed
Dunham, Katherine
University of Chicago Press, 280 pgs., $19.00
ISBN 0226171132

In this book, Dunham reveals how her anthropological research, her work in dance, and her fascination with the people and cults of Haiti worked their spell, catapulting her into experiences that she was often lucky to survive. Full of the flare and suspense of immersion in a strange and enchanting culture, *Island Possessed* is also a pioneering work in the anthropology of dance and a fascinating document on Haitian politics and voodoo.

Alvin Ailey: A Life in Dance
Dunning, Jennifer
DaCapo Press, 496 pgs., 1998, $21.00
ISBN 0306808250

Alvin Ailey was a choreographic giant in the modern dance world and a champion of African American talent and culture. Ailey's life and his work is chronicled in this biography by Jennifer Dunning, a *New York Times* dance critic who covered Ailey's career for twenty-five years. Based on his personal journals and hundreds of interviews with those who knew him, including Mikhail Baryshnikov, Judith Jamison, Leana Horne, Katherine Dunham, Sidney Poitier and Dustin Hoffman, *Alvin Ailey* is a moving story of a man who wove his life and culture into his dance.

BLACK DANCE: FROM 1619 TO TODAY
Emery, Lynne Fauley
Princeton Book Company, 397 pgs., 1989, $21.95
ISBN 0916622630

A complete history of black dance forms, including folk, ballet, jazz, tap, Broadway/Hollywood, disco and break dancing. Included are portraits of hundreds of black dancers and choreographers including Alvin Ailey, Katherine Dunham, Arthur Mitchell and Pearl Primus.

FROM HUCKLEBUCK TO HIP HOP: SOCIAL DANCE IN THE AFRICAN-AMERICAN COMMUNITY IN PHILADELPHIA
Roberts, John W.
Four-G Publishers, 123 pgs., 1997, $12.00
ISBN 0788137867

From Hucklebuck to Hip Hop consists of more than forty ethnographic interviews with African Americans to explore and document their memories and experiences of social dance and its role in community sociability. This book presents black social dance as a vital folk art form in South Philadelphia, Pennsylvania.

VITAL GRACE: THE BLACK MALE DANCER
Savio, Joanne, edited by Duane Cyrus
Edition Stemmle, 208 pgs., 1999, $22.70
ISBN 3908161312

Affirming the vital power of male dance, this collection of portraits by Joanne Savio, choreographed by Duane Cyrus, focuses on aspects often disregarded in views of the classical male dancer. Dance is a vital part of most cultures. History is passed down, courting is done and people are healed through dance ceremonies in which men take part. The artistic vision of *Vital Grace* is to inspire the viewer to appreciate the classic athletic agility of the male dancer.

THEATER

African Americans first began to perform in formerly all-white minstrel shows. Soon after they were producing black musicals written, produced and performed by all black performers. William Wells Brown wrote the first published black play, The Escape; or, a Leap for Freedom, in 1858.

Many black theater companies, such as the Ethiopian Art Theatre, were formed in the 1920s and 1930s, during the Harlem Renaissance. It was these black community theaters that gave actors like Ossie Davis and Ruby Dee an opportunity to develop their acting techniques. Black theater came into its own in the 1940s with the formation of the American Negro Theater and the Negro Playwrights' Company.

After World War II, as black theater grew more progressive, it became more militant. Plays like Lorraine Hansberry's A Raisin in the Sun brought attention to blacks and their struggles to maintain their identities in a color-conscious society.

With the 1960s came the birth of a new black theater, with playwrights like Amiri Baraka, who established the

Black Arts Repertory Theatre in Harlem. Black theater in the 1980s and beyond was dramatically influenced by such playwrights as August Wilson, Ntozake Shange, George C. Wolfe and Anna Devere Smith, whose works are supported by both black and white audiences.

COLORED CONTRADICTIONS: AN ANTHOLOGY OF CONTEMPORARY AFRICAN-AMERICAN PLAYS
Elam, Harry J., and Robert Alexander, eds.
Plume, 656 pgs., 1996, $17.95
ISBN 0452274974

In this collection, Elam and Alexander present twelve contemporary plays by famous African American playwrights written and produced in the 1990s, including *Shakin' the Mess Outta Misery* by Shay Youngblood, *For Black Boys Who Have Considered Homicide* by Keith Antar Mason, and *Imperceptible Mutabilities in the Third Kingdom* by Suzan Lori-Parks.

BLACK THEATRE USA: PLAYS BY AFRICAN AMERICANS
Hatch, James V., and Ted Shine, eds.
The Early Period 1847–1938: *Free Press, 432 pgs., 1996, $25.00*
ISBN 068482308X
The Recent Period 1935–Today: *Free Press, 528 pgs., 1996, $25.00*
ISBN 0684823071

Black Theatre USA is a collection of fifty-one outstanding plays written from 1847 to 1992, including the great names in the African American pantheon of writers, beginning with William Wells Brown's *The Escape; or, a Leap for Freedom*. These editions feature previously unpublished works as well as commercial successes such as George C. Wolfe's *The Colored Museum* and Charles Fuller's *A Soldier's Play*. Included are lesser-known masterpieces like Ben Caldwell's *The First Militant Preacher* and Owen Dodson's *The Confession Stone* and contemporary plays by women such as Robbie McCauley's *Sally's Rape* and Anna Devere Smith's *Fires in the Mirror*.

THE IMPACT OF RACE: THEATRE AND CULTURE
King, Woodie, Jr.
Applause Books, 300 pgs., 2003, $26.95
ISBN 1557835799

Woodie King explores the politics of art, the funding for black organizations, the critics' reviews of black theatre, and the way in which awards are handed out. *The Impact of Race* provides readers with a mosaic of current thinking in black culture.

THE NATIONAL BLACK DRAMA ANTHOLOGY: ELEVEN PLAYS FROM AMERICA'S LEADING AFRICAN-AMERICAN THEATERS
King, Woodie, Jr.
Applause Books, 536 pgs., 1996, $18.95
ISBN 1557832196

This wide-ranging anthology, edited by the founder of the New Federal Theater, celebrates the work of that company's black-owned, black-run peers by presenting works by eleven dramatists. Among the most interesting are Jeff Stetson's *The Meeting*, which imagines a meeting between Malcolm X and Martin Luther King Jr., and Shauneille Perry's updating of *In Dahomey*, the 1903 musical that was the first all-black show on Broadway.

FILM

The Birth of a Race, *produced by Emmett J. Scott in 1918, was the first independent black film ever released. It failed at the box office. In 1916, Noble and George Johnson formed the Lincoln Motion Picture Company, and after five marginally successful films, including* By Right of Birth, *the company folded in 1921.*

The first important black filmmaker to find black audiences was Oscar Micheaux. In 1918, Micheaux, a successful author, turned his novel The Homesteader *into a 35mm film. Catering to black audiences across the country, Micheaux has been credited with keeping the black independent film industry alive from 1918 until 1948.*

In the 1950s the film industry began to integrate blacks into roles that were more realistic and less racially offensive. This era brought to the forefront such notable African American actors as Sidney Poitier, Dorothy Dandridge, Canada Lee and Ethel Waters, among others. By the seventies blacks were a familiar part of the moviegoing experience. Actors like Ossie Davis and Melvin Van Peebles began to produce and direct films that were aimed at African American audiences. These early pioneers in film paved the way for Spike Lee, John Singleton, Julie Dash and Charles Burnett to create films that speak directly to the heart of the black experience.

Toms, Coons, Mulattoes, Mammies, and Bucks: An Interpretive History of Blacks in American Films
Bogle, Donald
Continuum International Publishing Group, 480 pgs., 2001, $22.95
ISBN 082641267X

This classic study of black images in American motion pictures has once again been completely revised and updated. It includes new sections on the end of the 1980s plus a chapter devoted to the unequaled rise of the new African American cinema and stars of the 1990s. Donald Bogie reveals the way in which the image of blacks in American movies has changed—and also the shocking way in which it has remained the same.

African-American Screenwriters Now: Conversations with Hollywood's Black Pack
Harris, Erich Leon
Silman-James Press, 277 pgs., 1996, $16.95
ISBN 1879505282

African American Screenwriters Now brings together interviews with both up-and-coming and established screenwriters, some of whom also work as directors and producers, and paints a vivid picture of the opportunities and obstacles that face today's black filmmakers in Hollywood. These writers discuss their influences, their goals, the birth of stories, the writing process, getting work and getting films made, alongside their comments on racial barriers and the portrayal of blacks in film.

Black Cinema Treasures: Lost and Found
Jones, G. William
University of North Texas Press, 242 pgs., 1997, $17.95
ISBN 1574410288

G. William Jones discovered and restored a collection of black films, known as the Tyler, Texas, Collection, in a warehouse in Tyler, Texas. The newly discovered films covered the black experience from the 1920s through the 1950s. These films—produced, written and directed by blacks—were made for blacks with all-black casts. Jones's discovery was a landmark in black cinematic history.

BLACK CITY CINEMA: AFRICAN AMERICAN URBAN EXPERIENCES IN FILM
Massood, Paula J.
Temple University Press, 280 pgs., 2003, $19.95
ISBN 1592130038

In *Black City Cinema*, Paula Massood shows how popular films reflected the massive social changes that resulted from the Great Migration of African Americans from the rural South to cities in the North, West and Midwest during the first three decades of the twentieth century. She considers the chief genres of African American and Hollywood narrative film: the black cast musicals of the 1920s and the "race" films of the early sound era to blaxploitation and 'hood films, as well as the work of Spike Lee toward the end of the century.

BLACKS IN BLACK AND WHITE: A SOURCE BOOK ON BLACK FILMS
Sampson, Henry T.
Scarecrow Press, 749 pgs., 1993, $94.00
ISBN 0810826054

Sampson traces the history of the black film industry from its beginnings around 1910 to its demise in 1950, chronicling the activities of pioneer black filmmakers and performers who have been virtually ignored by film historians. Significantly more information on Oscar Micheaux and other black producers of the period and descriptions of many more black films are included.

WHITE SCREENS/BLACK IMAGES: HOLLYWOOD FROM THE DARK SIDE
Snead, James
Routledge, 200 pgs., 1994, $24.95

ISBN 0415905745

White Screens/Black Images offers an array of film texts, drawn from both classical Hollywood cinema and black independent film culture. Individual chapters analyze *Birth of a Nation, King Kong,* Shirley Temple in *The Littlest Rebel* and *The Little Colonel,* Mae West in *I'm No Angel,* Marlene Dietrich in *Blonde Venus,* Bette Davis in *Jezebel,* the racism of Disney's *Song of the South,* and *Taxi Driver.*

TELEVISION

Of all the channels of mass communication, television is the most watched and most readily accessible, and often shapes the reality of those who have a limited worldview and accept what they see as unequivocal truth.

Television has always played a crucial role in how blacks are perceived. The earliest images of blacks on television were in domestic roles or as comic foils to white actors. While blacks graduated to their own shows, they did not control their images or characters—producers like Bill Cosby and a minority of actors/comics are the exception.

The African American's struggle against negative portrayals and images is a centuries-old struggle against oppression and discrimination. And television has played a major role in perpetuating the viewing of African Americans as second-class citizens.

PRIMETIME BLUES: AFRICAN AMERICANS ON NETWORK TELEVISION

Bogle, Donald
Farrar, Straus and Giroux, 448 pgs., 2001, $18.00
ISBN 0374527180

In *Primetime Blues,* the first comprehensive history of African Americans on network television, Donald Bogle traces the changing roles of African Americans on weekly prime time from the blatant stereotypes of television's early years to the more subtle stereotypes of recent eras. He also examines TV movies and miniseries such as *The Autobiography of Miss Jane Pittman* and *Roots.*

THE BLACK IMAGE IN THE WHITE MIND: MEDIA AND RACE IN AMERICA

Entman, Robert M., and Andrew Rojecki
University of Chicago Press, 320 pgs., 2001, $15.00
ISBN 0226210766

Using the media, and especially television, as barometers of race relations, Robert Entman and Andrew Rojecki explore and go beyond the treatment of African Americans on network and local news to uncover the messages sent about race by the entertainment industry—from prime-time dramas and sitcoms to commercials and Hollywood movies.

WATCHING RACE: TELEVISION AND THE STRUGGLE FOR "BLACKNESS"

Gray, Herman
University of Minnesota Press, 216 pgs., 1997, $16.95
ISBN 0816622515

Starting with the portrayal of blacks on series such as *The Jack Benny Show* and *Amos 'n' Andy*, Gray details the ongoing dialogue and struggle between television representations and cultural discourse to show how the meaning of blackness has changed through the years of the TV era. *Watching Race* examines how the political stakes, cultural perspectives and social locations of key cultural and social formations influence the representations and meanings of "blackness" in television.

SPECIAL COLLECTIONS

$\mathcal{T}$he books featured in this chapter are the ones that I've enjoyed time and again and recommend to family and friends to begin their special collections. Some are very plain in appearance, but inside you will discover a treasure. These are books that can be given for special occasions like birthdays and graduations. I never lend these books to anyone!

I also like to collect books that have beautiful covers and photographs. Some of those listed here cry out to be displayed in artistic settings or featured on your coffee table. Some of them are expensive, but they are all beautiful, big and worth sharing with family and friends. I have a large collection of these books and rotate them on my coffee table or on top of my bookcases.

BLACK BEAUTY: A HISTORY AND A CELEBRATION
Arogundade, Ben
Thunder's Mouth Press, 192 pgs., 2001, $27.95
ISBN 156025341X

  Black Beauty is a visual history of blackness and beauty. Arogundade's subjects are the famous and the not-so-famous, representing the chronology of Western black beauty from the exhibited African Venus Hottentot in London and Paris to contemporary icons of beauty like Lauryn Hill and Tyson Beckwith. Their commonality is their blackness and uniqueness of beauty. With over 150 color and black-and-white photographs, *Black Beauty* discusses the position of blacks within the beauty hierarchy of the West, as well as the kinds of work available to black models within the past century. It also shows how the aesthetic of black beauty has changed over the years.

THE AFRICAN AMERICAN BOOK OF VALUES: CLASSIC MORAL STORIES
Barboza, Steven
Broadway Books, 960 pgs., 2003, $19.95
ISBN 0767912942

In the tradition of *The Book of Virtues*, Steven Barboza gathers together an impressive volume of poems, stories, letters, songs, folktales and short biographies that will help guide African Americans and others solidly and securely through life's moral and ethical dilemmas.

AFRICAN CEREMONIES
Beckwith, Carol, and Angela Fisher
Abrams, 744 pgs., 2000, $150.00
ISBN 0810942054

Carol Beckwith and Angela Fisher have spent the past ten years photographing the customs and rituals of African tribal cultures in twenty-six different countries. Many of the rituals and practices have never been documented, much less photographed by outsiders. The work is divided into cycles of life, beginning with birth and initiation through rituals of ancestral reverence and the final transition, death. There are close to 850 full-color photographs with accompanying commentary on each culture. This book is a beautiful work of art.

LIFT EVERY VOICE AND SING: A CELEBRATION OF THE NEGRO NATIONAL ANTHEM: 100 YEARS, 100 VOICES
Bond, Julian, and Sondra Kathryn Wilson, eds.
Random House, 256 pgs., 2000, $29.95
ISBN 0679463151

Poet and composer James Weldon Johnson and his brother J. Rosamond Johnson sat down in 1900 to write a song to commemorate Abraham Lincoln's birthday. It was to be sung by a chorus of five hundred black schoolchildren in Jacksonville, Florida. From Jacksonville, the song traveled all over the South. It became known as the Negro National Anthem and was sung throughout the United States. This book of photographs and essays reveals how deeply these words are imbedded in the consciousness of many African Americans.

THE MIDDLE PASSAGE: WHITE SHIPS BLACK CARGO
Feelings, Tom
Dial Books, 80 pgs., 1995, $50.00

ISBN 0803718047

Tom Feelings spent twenty years illustrating the horror and pain of the Middle Passage—the journey our enslaved ancestors began across the Atlantic Ocean. The images are in black-and-white, blurred, elongated and narrow, which heightens the sense of the cramped spaces this human cargo occupied. The haunting illustrations depict women mourning for their babies; women being raped and abused by the slavers; bodies that are no longer useful being thrown overboard to the sharks; Africans who refused to eat being force-fed. This is the real story of our ancestors' odyssey to the New World.

AFRICANA: THE ENCYCLOPEDIA OF THE AFRICAN AND AFRICAN AMERICAN EXPERIENCE

Gates, Henry Louis, Jr., and Kwame Anthony Appiah, eds.
Basic Civitas Books, 2,144 pgs., 1999, $59.95
ISBN 0465000711

W.E.B. Du Bois set out in 1909 to create an encyclopedia for the African world and the African diaspora. It was left unfinished at the time of his death in 1963. Thirty-six years after Du Bois's death, Henry Louis Gates Jr. and Kwame Anthony Appiah undertook this project based on Du Bois's model. The book contains 3,500 entries from 220 contributors like Evelyn Brooks Higginbotham, David Levering Lewis and Cornel West. Maps, tables, photographs and charts accompany articles on the history of African nations. Also included are cultural, political and religious movements in Africa and the diaspora.

KING: THE PHOTOBIOGRAPHY OF MARTIN LUTHER KING, JR.

Johnson, Charles, Bob Adelman, and Robert Phelan, eds.
Viking Press, 288 pgs., 2000, $40.00
ISBN 0670892165

King is a powerful collection of photographic images edited by photographers Bob Adelman and Robert Phelan, combined with text by writer Charles Johnson, that details the pivotal events of King's public and family life in a rich and stirring format. In this book we see Martin Luther King Jr. in all his aspects: as son and student, husband and father, powerful preacher and courageous leader of the Civil Rights movement, martyr for the cause of racial justice and finally American icon.

FREEDOM: A PHOTOGRAPHIC HISTORY OF THE AFRICAN AMERICAN STRUGGLE
Marable, Manning, and Leith Mullings, eds.
Phaidon, 512 pgs., 2003, $9.95
ISBN 0714842702

This photographic journey of the African American struggle for equality begins with abolitionists like Harriet Tubman, who escaped slavery in 1849 and then helped others to freedom, and continues to the present. *Freedom* chronicles the battle to eradicate slavery through the Civil War and, once slavery was officially outlawed, it traces the evolution of its dual legacy—segregation and racism. With five hundred striking black-and-white photographs and one hundred color photographs, *Freedom* tells of the tremendous courage, determination and power of a people fighting for a common goal.

ONE MORE RIVER TO CROSS: AN AFRICAN AMERICAN PHOTOGRAPH ALBUM
Myers, Walter Dean
Harcourt Brace & Company, 166 pgs., 1999, $18.00
ISBN 0152020217

Author Walter Dean Myers turns his eye to images of black America in a stunningly beautiful anthology of images, many of which are from his own collection. Myers allows the photographs to speak for themselves, without overwhelming text or commentary. Some of these photographs are visibly old and worn, but still contain the essence of their images. While many of these photographs are of black icons like Frederick Douglass and Madame C. J. Walker, others show lesser-known and unknown black Americans. Myers provides information on each of the photographs in the "Captions" section of the book.

FREEDOM'S CHILDREN: THE PASSAGE FROM EMANCIPATION TO THE GREAT MIGRATION
Thomas, Velma Maia
Crown, 32 pgs., 2000, $32.50
ISBN 0762869607

Freedom's Children is a multidimensional, interactive treasure chest. Thomas has given us an opportunity to hold in our own hands documents, books and letters of that perilous period in African American history right after emancipation and through the Great Migration out of the South. *Freedom's Children* documents the determination and valor of former slaves to take their place in the defining and shaping of black communities and institutions. It was a journey in which every step was met with deceit, opposition and violence.

THE FACE OF OUR PAST: IMAGES OF BLACK WOMEN FROM COLONIAL AMERICA TO THE PRESENT
Thompson, Kathleen, and Hilary Mac Austin, eds.
Indiana University Press, 258 pgs., 2000, $35.00
ISBN 025333635X

Of the images that previously have been presented in print, the majority have been of famous black women. *The Face of Our Past* brings the ordinary black woman to center stage, showing how she lives, loves her family, works to survive, fights for her people and expresses her individuality. In addition to 302 carefully chosen images, Kathleen Thompson and Hilary Mac Austin provide quotations from letters, diaries, journals and other sources.

REFLECTIONS IN BLACK: A HISTORY OF BLACK PHOTOGRAPHERS, 1840 TO THE PRESENT
Willis, Deborah
W.W. Norton, 368 pgs., 2002, $50.00
ISBN 0393322807

Many of us are familiar with the work of photographers James Van Der Zee, Carrie May Weems and John Mosley, but here we see, often for the first time, images captured by photographers who are not well known. These images document our history as a people in America from the last generation of slaves to the 1990s. Each photograph tells a story of a moment in time in black America. Deborah Willis has succeeded at the difficult task of collecting, collating and exhibiting the work of African American photographers from the 1840s to the present.

CHILDREN'S LITERATURE

*L*iteracy and knowledge go hand in hand. And they both begin at home. Why wait for your children to start school to learn how to read and learn about their heritage and the world around them? Children who have their own books will grow up with an appreciation and respect for the written word that will carry them a long way.

The field of children's literature has developed and grown over the past thirty years or so. Some authors and illustrators have also developed and grown over the years. With children's literature, the illustrations are just as important as the words. Together they weave stories that have dimensions of sight and sound.

To make certain that I presented the best in children's literature, I enlisted the help of Natalie A. Marshall, M.Ed., a children's literacy consultant, to compile the books in this section. These books constitute the basics of a good children's library. While many are picture books and storybooks, there are also chapter books that are geared to young adult readers. Although these books are specifically written for children, adults can learn a lot by reading them with their children.

WHY MOSQUITOES BUZZ IN PEOPLE'S EARS: A WEST AFRICAN TALE
Aardema, Verna, illustrated by Leo and Diane Dillon
Puffin, 32 pgs., 1999, $6.99
ISBN 0140549056

A retelling of a traditional West African tale that reveals how a mosquito's lie sets off a series of reactions in the jungle that results in the owl's refusal to wake the sun and the lion's decision to call a meeting of the animals.

BIGMAMA'S
Crews, Donald
Green Willow, 40 pgs., 1998, $5.95
ISBN 0688158420

"Cottondale! Cottondale!" called the conductor. They had arrived. The summer at Bigmama's house in Florida had begun for young Donald Crews and his family. Everything was always just the same, inside and out. There was the house to check out and the farm to explore. And best of all, there were cousins and friends and family to talk to and play with through the hot, endless, wonderful days of summer.

The Hatseller and the Monkeys: A West African Folk Tale

Diakite, Baba Wague
Scholastic, 32 pgs., 1999, $15.95
ISBN 0590960695

Everyone familiar with the popular story "Caps for Sale" will immediately recognize this authentic African tale. Readers will love the mischievous monkeys that steal the peddler's caps. And they will laugh at the monkeys' funny antics as the peddler outsmarts them and gets his caps back.

Jambo Means Hello: Swahili Alphabet Book

Feelings, Muriel, illustrated by Tom Feelings
Puffin, 56 pgs., 1981, $6.99
ISBN 0140546529

Muriel and Tom Feelings, author and illustrator of the Caldecott Honor Book *Moja Means One: Swahili Counting Book*, have now collaborated on a companion volume—a Swahili alphabet book. Selecting twenty-four words, one for each letter of the Swahili alphabet, *Jambo Means Hello* gives children a simple lesson in the Swahili language while familiarizing them with some important aspects of traditional East African life. Illustrator Tom Feelings has provided a beautifully detailed double-spread painting for each letter. A map of Africa showing the countries where Swahili is spoken is also included.

The Patchwork Quilt

Flournoy, Valerie, illustrated by Jerry Pinkney
Dial, 32 pgs., 1985, $16.99
ISBN 0803700970

Tanya loved listening to her grandmother talk about the patchwork quilt as she cut and stitched together the pieces of colorful fabric. A scrap of blue from brother Jim's favorite old pants, a piece of gold left over from Mama's Christmas dress, a bright square from Tanya's Halloween costume—all are fit together to make a quilt of memories. But then one day Tanya's grandmother becomes ill, and Tanya doesn't know how to help her. It's then that she decides to finish Grandma's masterpiece herself, and with the help of Mama and the whole family, she sets to work.

HONEY, I LOVE AND OTHER LOVE POEMS
Greenfield, Eloise, illustrated by Leo and Diane Dillon
Harper Trophy, 46 pgs., 1986, $5.99
ISBN 0064430979

Each of these sixteen love poems is spoken straight from the heart of a child. Riding on a train, listening to music, playing with a friend . . . each poem elicits a new appreciation of the rich content of everyday life. And each poem is accompanied by a beautiful drawing, both portrait and panoramic, that deepens the insights contained in the singing words.

THE VILLAGE OF ROUND AND SQUARE HOUSES
Grifalconi, Ann
Little, Brown, 32 pgs., 1986, $16.95
ISBN 0316328626

The village of Tos is like no other village in the world, for in this village the women live in round houses and the men live in square ones. The story of how this came to be is told from the point of view of a young girl who grew up there. Ann Grifalconi's bold, dynamic art and her rhythmic storytelling make this a perfect book for reading aloud.

MEET DANITRA BROWN
Grimes, Nikki, illustrated by Floyd Cooper
Mulberry Books, 32 pgs., 1997, $6.99
ISBN 0688154719

Zuri Jackson introduces us to her best friend, Danitra Brown, a truly remarkable girl, who wears only purple because she might be a princess, faces down bullies, rides her bike as if it had wings—and is definitely going to win the Nobel Prize one day.

A STORY, A STORY: AN AFRICAN TALE
Haley, Gail E.
Aladdin, 36 pgs., 1988, $6.99

ISBN 0689712014

Once, all the stories in the world belonged to Nyame, the Sky God. He kept them in a box beside his throne. But Anansi, the spider-man, wanted them—and caught three sly creatures to get them. This story of how we got our own stories to tell is adapted from an African folktale. Gail E. Haley received the Caldecott Medal for this book.

THE PEOPLE COULD FLY: AMERICAN BLACK FOLKTALES
Hamilton, Virginia, illustrated by Leo and Diane Dillon
Alfred A. Knopf, 192 pgs., 1993, $13.00
ISBN 0679843361

"These tales were created out of sorrow. But the hearts and minds of the black people who formed them, expanded them, and passed them on to us were full of love and hope. We must look on the tales as a celebration of the human spirit. Remember the voices from the past. As do the folktales, keep close all the past that was good, and that remains full of promise." —Virginia Hamilton

NAPPY HAIR
Herron, Carolivia, illustrated by Joe Cepeda
Dragonfly Books, 32 pgs., 1998, $6.99
ISBN 0679894454

In a unique and vibrant picture book that uses the African American call-and-response tradition, a family talks back and forth about adorable Brenda's hair—it's the nappiest, the curliest, the twistiest hair in the whole family. The family delights in poking gentle fun with their hilarious descriptions, all the time discovering the beauty and meaning of Brenda's hair.

AMAZING GRACE
Hoffman, Mary, illustrated by Caroline Binch
Dial, 32 pgs., 1991, $16.99
ISBN 0803710402

When there's the chance to get a part in the school production of *Peter Pan*, Grace knows that the part of Peter is made for her.

Grace proves that she can do anything despite the fact that she is a girl—and black.

SWEET CLARA AND THE FREEDOM QUILT
Hopkinson, Deborah, illustrated by James Ransome
Dragonfly Books, 32 pgs., 1995, $6.99
ISBN 0679874720

Clara, a slave and seamstress on the Home Plantation, knows that the Underground Railroad can lead her to freedom. The only problem is how to find it. By piecing together scraps of cloth with scraps of information gathered from other slaves, she fashions a map so secret that even the master won't suspect.

HOW MANY STARS IN THE SKY?
Hort, Lenny, illustrated by James Ransome
Mulberry Books, 32 pgs., 1997, $5.99
ISBN 068815218X

Mama's away one night, and her son can't sleep. He tries to relax by counting stars, but the more he sees, the more determined he is to count every single one. Then the son finds that Daddy can't sleep either. Together, the two of them set off on an unforgettable all-night journey of discovery.

AUNT FLOSSIE'S HATS (AND CRAB CAKES LATER)
Howard, Elizabeth Fitzgerald, illustrated by James Ransome
Clarion Books, 32 pgs., 1995, $6.95
ISBN 039572077X

Sunday afternoons are Sarah and Susan's favorite time of the week. That's when they visit their great-great-aunt Flossie and hear the stories she has to tell about the days of long ago, when she was young. This tender and loving book is a joyful encounter of the elder and younger generations—a story for family sharing, again and again.

Bright Eyes, Brown Skin

Hudson, Cheryl Willis, illustrated by Bernette G. and George Ford
Just Us Books, 32 pgs., 1990, $6.95
ISBN 0940975238

Four children who feel good about who they are and how they look enjoy the activities of a typical day at school, happy and brimming with confidence and self-esteem.

Do Like Kyla

Johnson, Angela, illustrated by James Ransome
Scholastic, 32 pgs., 1993, $6.95
ISBN 0531070409

From the moment they wake up, Kyla takes the lead and her little sister follows. She longs to do everything Kyla does, whether it's tapping at the birds in the windows, kissing the sunbeam on the dog's head, or crunching through the snow in purple boots. All day long, Kyla is patient with her tagalong. Finally, in the evening, when the birds gather again at the window, something new happens between follower and leader.

The Snowy Day

Keats, Ezra Jack
Puffin, 32 pgs., 1976, $5.99
ISBN 0140501827

The Snowy Day captures the magic of the first snowfall. Universal in its appeal, the story has become a favorite of millions and reveals a child's wonder at a new world and the hope of capturing and keeping that wonder forever.

Wood-Hoopoe Willie

Kroll, Virginia, illustrated by Katherine Roundtree
Charlesbridge Publishing, 32 pgs., 1995, $6.95
ISBN 0881064084

Willie makes music every chance he gets. He will use anything to create the sounds of the rhythms he feels inside him. Willie dreams of playing the African instruments of his ancestors, that his grandpa describes. The Kwanzaa festival and the encouragement of his grandfather provide the chance for Willie to live out his dreams. Color illustrations.

SAM AND THE TIGERS
Lester, Julius, illustrated by Jerry Pinkney
Puffin, 40 pgs., 2000, $6.99
ISBN 0140562885

"Once upon a time there was a place called Sam-sam-sa-mara, where the animals and the people lived and worked together like they didn't know they weren't supposed to. There was a little boy in Sam-sam-sa-mara named Sam . . ." So begins Julius Lester's delightful new telling of one of the most controversial books in children's literature, Helen Bannerman's *Little Black Sambo*.

THE HUNDRED PENNY BOX
Mathis, Sharon Bell, illustrated by Leo and Diane Dillon
Puffin, 48 pgs., 1986, $5.99
ISBN 0140321691

Michael's great-great-aunt Dew was a hundred years old, and she kept an old box filled with pennies, one for each birthday. Michael's mother wanted to throw out the old box and buy a new one, but Aunt Dew said, "Anybody takes my hundred penny box, takes me." And, for his love for Aunt Dew, Michael knew he had to try to save the hundred penny box that contained all the stories of her life.

ANANSI THE SPIDER: A TALE FROM THE ASHANTI
McDermott, Gerald
Henry Holt & Company, Inc., 48 pgs., 1987, $6.95
ISBN 0805003118

In this traditional tale from West Africa, Anansi, the Spider, sets out on a long journey. Threatened by Fish and Falcon, he is saved from terrible fates by his sons. But which of his six sons should he reward? The color, the splendid design montage and the authentic African language rhythms forge a new direction in picture books for children.

In the Hollow of Your Hand: Slave Lullabies
McGill, Alice, illustrated by Michael Cummings
Houghton Mifflin, 40 pgs., 2000, $18.00 with companion CD
ISBN 0395857554

Slave lullabies, created from the African American experience, were sung to give hope for a better time to come. Even though these lullabies were born of hardship and overwhelming sadness, they can be thought of as musical stories for children and adults. Here they are preserved along with vibrant quilt collages and a companion CD.

Mirandy and Brother Wind
McKissack, Patricia, illustrated by Jerry Pinkney
Dragonfly Books, 32 pgs., 1997, $6.99
ISBN 0679883339

With the junior cakewalk fast approaching, Mirandy is determined to capture the best partner for the dance. And who is the best partner? The wind, of course! But as Grandmama Beasley says, "Can't nobody put shackles on Brother Wind, chile. He be special. He be free."

The Black Snowman
Mendez, Phil, illustrated by Carole Byard
Scholastic, 48 pgs., 1991, $5.99
ISBN 0590448730

Through the powers of a magical kente, a black snowman comes to life and helps young Jacob discover the beauty of his black heritage as well as his own self-worth.

Uncle Jed's Barbershop
Mitchell, Margaree King, illustrated by James Ransome
Aladdin, 40 pgs., 1998, $6.99
ISBN 0689819137

In the segregated South of the 1920s, Uncle Jed was the only black barber in a county of sharecroppers, but he always dreamed of owning his own barbershop. Finally, on his seventy-ninth birthday, Uncle Jed opens the doors of his new shop.

THE ORPHAN BOY
Mollel, Tololwa M., illustrated by Paul Morin
Clarion Books, 34 pgs., 1995, $6.95
ISBN 0395720796

The old man is searching the sky for a familiar star, when suddenly a boy appears out of the darkness. Happy to have a son at last, the old man welcomes Kileken into his compound. In this tale from his homeland, Tololwa M. Mollel explains why the planet Venus is known to the Masai as Kileken, the orphan boy.

ASHANTI TO ZULU: AFRICAN TRADITIONS
Musgrove, Margaret W., illustrated by Leo and Diane Dillon
Puffin, 32 pgs., 1992, $6.99
ISBN 0140546049

From A to Z, an authentic portrait of twenty-six African tribes, stunningly illustrated by winners of the 1976 and 1977 Caldecott Medal.

A IS FOR AFRICA
Onyefulu, Ifeoma
Puffin, 32 pgs., 1997, $5.99
ISBN 0140562222

"D is for Drums used to make music." "N is for Neighbors, passing on the latest news." "W is for weaving, a craft parents teach to their children." The stunning photographs were taken in Nigeria where the author/photographer grew up. The images pictured represent the warm family ties and traditional village life found throughout this vast, colorful continent.

DUKE ELLINGTON: THE PIANO PRINCE AND HIS ORCHESTRA
Pinkney, Andrea Davis, illustrated by Brian Pinkney
Hyperion Books for Children, 32 pgs., 1998, $15.95

ISBN 0786801786

His name was Duke. Duke Ellington. As a child, he said the piano made an *umpy-dump* sound that was headed nowhere worth following. But years later he heard the piano played a whole new way. People called the music "ragtime," and soon the sound had Duke's fingers riding the piano keys. This is the story of one of the greatest composers of the twentieth century, the king of the keys, Duke Ellington.

Max Found Two Sticks
Pinkney, Brian
Aladdin Books, 40 pgs., 1997, $6.99
ISBN 068981593X

On a day when Max doesn't feel too much like talking to anybody, he finds two sticks that make a perfect pair of drumsticks. Max learns that you don't need to talk to say how you feel, especially when you've got music!

Back Home
Pinkney, Gloria Jean, illustrated by Jerry Pinkney
Puffin, 40 pgs., 1999, $6.99
ISBN 0140565477

Even though eight-year-old Ernestine lives with her family up North, "back home" is Lumberton, North Carolina, the place where she was born and where her mama grew up. From the moment she steps off the train, Ernestine feels right at home in the lush, green countryside, working on the family farm and spending time with her aunt, uncle and cousins.

Aïda
Price, Leontyne, illustrated by Leo and Diane Dillon
Harcourt Trade, 32 pgs., 1997, $8.00
ISBN 0152015469

Opera star Leontyne Price retells the story of this famous opera about the beautiful princess of Ethiopia.

TAR BEACH
Ringgold, Faith
Dragonfly Books, 32 pgs., 1996, $6.99
ISBN 0517885441

Cassie Louise Lightfoot, eight years old in 1939, has a dream: to be free to go wherever she wants for the rest of her life. One night, up on "tar beach"—the rooftop of her family's Harlem apartment building—her dream comes true. This magical story resonates with a universal wish. *Tar Beach* is a seamless weaving of fiction, autobiography and African American history and literature.

SUKEY AND THE MERMAID
San Souci, Robert D., illustrated by Brian Pinkney
Aladdin, 32 pgs., 1996, $6.99
ISBN 068980718X

A girl named Sukey lived with her ma and new step pa, whom Sukey called "Mister Hard-Times." Every day, while he watched, she hoed the weeds in the garden and every day she sang: "Mister Hard-Times / Since you come / My ma don't like me / My work never done." One morning, when her step pa wasn't looking, Sukey ran away to her secret hiding place by the sea and unwittingly called up Mama Jo, a beautiful black mermaid. The adventures that followed changed her life forever.

ABIYOYO: BASED ON A SOUTH AFRICAN LULLABY AND FOLK STORY
Seeger, Pete, illustrated by Michael Hays
Aladdin, 48 pgs., 1994, $6.99 with companion CD
ISBN 0689718101

Once there was a little boy who played the ukelele. Wherever he'd go, he'd make things disappear. Soon the townspeople grew tired of the boy's noise and his father's tricks, and banished both of them to the edge of town. There they lived until one day the terrible giant Abiyoyo appeared. He was as tall as a tree, and it was said that he could eat people up. Everyone was terrified except the boy and his father, and they came up with a plan to save the town. This edition includes a CD of two different versions of "Abiyoyo."

Mufaro's Beautiful Daughters: An African Tale
Steptoe, John
HarperCollins Children's Books, 32 pgs., 1987, $16.89
ISBN 0688040462

Everyone agreed that Mufaro's two daughters Nyasha and Manyara were very beautiful, but they were also very different: Nyasha was kind but Manyara was selfish, bad-tempered and spoiled. When the king decided to take a wife Mufaro declared that only the king could choose between Nyasha and Manyara. Manyara set out to make certain that she would be chosen. In *Mufaro's Beautiful Daughters*, John Steptoe has created a memorable modern fable of pride going before a fall with stunning paintings that glow with the beauty, warmth and internal vision of the land and people of his ancestors.

Working Cotton
Williams, Sherley Anne, illustrated by Carole Byard
Harcourt Trade, 32 pgs., 1997, $7.00
ISBN 0152014829

The bus arrives at the field in the dark of morning, workers gather around the fire and everyone speaks in smoky whispers. Shelan's family's day in the field begins. Too small to carry her own sack, Shelan piles cotton in the middle of the row for her mamma to collect. She admires her daddy who picks cotton so fast you can hardly see him do it; and she imagines how much cotton she could pick if she were as old as her sisters.

Sundiata: Lion King of Mali
Wisniewski, David
Houghton Mifflin, 32 pgs., 1999, $6.95
ISBN 0395764815

In the thirteenth century, Sundiata overcame physical handicaps, social disgrace and strong opposition to rule the West African trading empire of Mali.

CORNROWS
Yarbrough, Camille, illustrated by Carole Byard
Putnam Publishing Group, 48 pgs., 1997, $6.99
ISBN 0698114361
    This book explains how the hairstyle of cornrows, a symbol of Africa since ancient times, can today, in the United States, symbolize the courage of outstanding African Americans.

How to Purchase These Books

The books listed here can be purchased at your local bookstore. If they don't have the book you want, ask if they will order it for you. If you have Internet access, you can go to www.mosaic.com for a listing of African American booksellers in your area, or you can go to one of the major chains' websites for ordering information.

Online Book Resources

INDEPENDENT BLACK BOOKSELLERS
www.aalbc.com
www.angelsbookstore.com
www.cushcity.com
www.jokaes.com
www.mosaic.com

MAJOR BOOK CHAINS
www.amazon.com
www.barnesandnoble.com
Borders Books has teamed with Amazon.com

AMERICAN BOOKSELLERS' DIRECTORY OF AMERICAN BOOKSTORES
www.bookweb.org/bookstores/usa_states.html

DIRECTORY OF INTERNATIONAL BOOKSTORES
www.bookweb.org/bookstores/international.html

Online Book Retailers Price Comparison and Search Sites
www.bestwebbuys.com/books/stores
www.allbookstores.com
www.addall.com

Search by ISBN and Price Comparison
www.isbn.nu/welcome.html

AUTHOR INDEX

— A —

Aardema, Verna specializes in the modernization and adaptation of traditional African folktales. She is the author of numerous children's books, including *Tales from the Story Hat*, *Why Mosquitos Buzz in People's Ears*, *This for That: A Tongi Tale* and *Anasi Does the Impossible: An Ashanti Tale*.

Adisa, Opal Palmer is a writer, literary critic and storyteller. She is a professor in the Ethnic Studies/Cultural Diversity Program at the California College of Arts and Crafts. Her books include *It Begins with Tears*, *Tamarind and Mango Women* and *Leaf-of-Life*.

Adoff, Arnold is a poet, anthropologist and the author of more than thirty books for young people. His books include *I Am the Darker Brother: An Anthology of Modern Poems by African Americans* and *Love Letters*.

Akbar, Na'im is a psychologist and author of several books, including *Breaking the Chains of Psychological Slavery*, *Visions for Black Men*, *The Community of Self* and *Know Thy Self*. He is CEO of Na'im Akbar Consultants and president of Mind Publications and Associates.

Alcena, Valiere is a clinical professor at Albert Einstein College of Medicine, Yeshiva University, and adjunct professor of medicine at New York Medical College. His work includes *The African American Health Book*, *African American Woman's Health Book* and *The Expanding Epidemic: What the Public Needs to Know*.

Allen, James is an Atlanta antiques dealer who spent over a decade collecting more than 150 lynching photos, culminating in an exhibit of his collection at the New York Historical Society.

Anderson, Leslie Kent is an assistant professor of Women's Studies at Oglethorpe University. She wrote *Woman of Color, Daughter of Privilege: Amanda Anderson Dickerson 1848–1893*, the true story of a slave who became the wealthiest black woman in the South.

Andrews, Raymond (1934–1991) was the winner of the first James Baldwin Prize for Fiction in 1978 for *Appalachee Red*. He worked a variety of jobs while writing his trilogy of stories about the lives of rural blacks in the Georgia Piedmont region. His other books include *Rosibelle Lee Wildcat Tennessee Baby Sweets*, *Jessie and Jesus and Cousin Claire* and *The Last Radio Baby: A Memoir*.

Andrews, William L. is a literary historian, critic and English professor at University of North Carolina at Chapel Hill. He was series editor for the *North American Slave Narratives, Beginnings to 1920*, a database and electronic text project with the Academic Affairs Library of UNC–Chapel Hill. He coedited (with Henry Louis Gates Jr.) *Slave Narratives* and *Pioneers of the Black Atlantic*.

Angelou, Maya is an author, inaugural poet, playwright, editor, actress, director and teacher. She holds the lifetime position as the first Reynolds Professor of American Studies at Wake Forest University and is the author of many books, including *I Know Why the Caged Bird Sings*, *All God's Children Need Traveling Shoes* and *A Song Flung Up to Heaven*.

Ansa, Tina McElroy is the author of several novels, including *Baby of the Family*, *Ugly Ways*, *The Hand I Fan With* and *You Know Better*.

Aptheker, Herbert (1915–2003) was a historian of the African American experience. Among his most prominent works are *American Negro Slave Revolts* and the three-volume *Documentary History of the Negro People in the United States*.

Arogundade, Ben is an architect, model, journalist and the author of *Black Beauty: A History and a Celebration*.

Ashe, Arthur (1943–1993) was one of the most prominent tennis players of his time. In 1975 he won Wimbledon and then went on to win three Grand Slams during his career. He achieved number one ranking in the world. He is the author (with Arnold Rampersad) of *Days of Grace: A Memoir*.

— B —

Bailey, Cornelia Walker is an author, lecturer and tour guide at Sapelo Island, on the Georgia Sea Coast. Walker is a descendant of African slaves taken from Senegal, Sierra Leone and Liberia. Her autobiography (with Christena Bledsoe) is *God, Dr. Buzzard and the Bolito Man*.

Baker, Jean-Claude is one of Josephine Baker's adopted children. He coauthored (with Chris Chase) her biography, *Josephine: The Hungry Heart*.

Baldwin, James (1924–1987) was a writer, noted for his novels on sexual and personal identity, and his sharp essays on the Civil Rights struggle in the United States. He is the author of *Go Tell It on the Mountain*, *Giovanni's Room* and *If Beale Street Could Talk*.

Ball, Edward is a descendant of a seventeenth-century plantation owner in Charleston, South Carolina. He is the author of *Slaves in the Family* and *The Sweet Hell Inside*.

Bambara, Toni Cade (1939–1995) was a noted writer, editor, teacher and educator. She left a legacy of her own work through her short stories collected in *Gorilla, My Love* and *The Sea Birds Are Still Alive* and the novel *The Salt Eaters*.

Barboza, Steven has authored numerous books, including *The African American Book of Values: Classic Moral Stories, I Feel Like Dancing* and *Sugar Hill*.

Bauerlein, Mark is a professor at Emory University in the Department of English. He is the author of *Negrophobia: A Race Riot in Atlanta, 1906*.

Beckwith, Carol is an anthropological photographer who, with Angela Fisher, has traveled all over Africa for the past thirty years. Their works include *African Ceremonies, Passages: Photographs in Africa* and *African Ark: People and Ancient Cultures of Ethiopia and the Horn of Africa*.

Bell, Derrick A. is a civil rights activist, law scholar and professor at New York University. He is the author of *Faces at the Bottom of the Well, And We Are Not Saved* and many others.

Bell, Madison Smartt is the author of nine novels, including *All Souls' Rising, The Washington Square Ensemble, Waiting for the End of the World* and *Straight Cut*. Bell has also published two collections of short stories, *Zero Db and Other Stories* and *Barking Man*.

Bennett, Lerone, Jr. is a writer, social historian and executive editor of *Ebony* magazine. His books include *Before the Mayflower: A History of Black America* and *Forced into Glory: Abraham Lincoln's White Dream*.

Berlin, Ira is a professor of History at the University of Maryland. He is the author of *Many Thousands Gone: The First Two Centuries of Slavery in Northern America* and editor of *Remembering Slavery: African Americans Talk About Their Personal Experiences of Slavery and Emancipation.*

Bogle, Donald is an authority on African Americans in film. He is the author of *Toms, Coons, Mulattoes, Mammies, and Bucks: An Interpretive History of Blacks in American Films, Primetime Blues: African Americans on Network Television* and *Dorothy Dandridge: A Biography.* Bogle teaches at the University of Pennsylvania and New York University.

Bond, Julian was a founder of the Student Nonviolent Coordinating Committee (SNCC) and was elected in 1965 to the Georgia House of Representatives. He is currently a Professor of History at the University of Virginia and Chairman of the Board of the NAACP. Bond is coeditor (with scholar Sondra K. Wilson) of *Lift Every Voice and Sing: A Celebration of the Negro National Anthem: 100 Years, 100 Voices.*

Bontemps, Arna Wendell (1902–1973) was one of the most important writers of the Harlem Renaissance era. He was an anthologist, collaborator, teacher and writer. His books include *100 Years of Negro Freedom* and *American Negro Poetry: An Anthology.*

Boyd, Herb is the national editor of *The Black World Today* (TBWT), an award-winning journalist, educator and author of many books, including *Brotherman: The Odyssey of Black Men in America.*

Boyd, Valerie is an arts editor and book critic at the *Atlanta Journal-Constitution.* She is the author of *Wrapped in Rainbows: The Life of Zora Neale Hurston.*

Branch, Taylor is a Pulitzer Prize–winning historian and author of a trilogy on the Civil Rights movement that includes *Parting the*

Waters: America in the King Years 1954–63 and *Pillar of Fire: America in the King Years 1963–65.*

Brinkley, Douglas is director of the Eisenhower Center for American Studies and a professor of History at the University of New Orleans. He is the author of *Rosa Parks* and *12 Million Black Voices.*

Brooks, Gwendolyn (1917–2000) was one of the major modern poets and the first African American writer to win a Pulitzer Prize, for *Annie Allen.* She is best known for her sensitive portraits of urban blacks who encounter racism and poverty in their daily lives. She authored several collections of poetry, including *A Street in Bronzeville, Children Coming Home* and *In the Mecca.*

Brown, Claude (1927–2002) was an African American writer and children's advocate. He is the author of *Manchild in the Promised Land*, his best-selling autobiography about his youth in Harlem, New York, and *The Children of Ham*, a story about struggling young blacks in Harlem.

Brown, Elaine is a writer, civil rights activist and former leader of the Black Panther Party. Brown works with Mothers Advocating Juvenile Justice, to free incarcerated children, and the Legal Defense Committee for Michael "Little B" Lewis. She is the author of an autobiography, *A Taste of Power: A Black Woman's Story* and *The Condemnation of Little B.*

Brown, Wesley is a professor of English at Rutgers University and the author of *Tragic Magic, Darktown Strutters* and the forthcoming *Push Comes to Shove.* He has written three plays and coedited the multicultural anthology *Imagining America: Stories from the Promised Land.*

Brown, William Wells (1815–1884) was a former slave and abolitionist leader known for writing the first travel book and the first play to be published by an African American. He is the author of

From Fugitive Slave to Free Man: The Autobiographies of William Wells Brown.

Bundles, A'Lelia is a television news journalist and the author of her great-great-grandmother's biography, *On Her Own Ground: The Life and Times of Madam C. J. Walker.*

Burns, Ken is a jazz historian and award-winning documentary filmmaker. His films include *The Civil War, Baseball* and *Jazz.*

Butler, Octavia is a noted African American science fiction writer who has written many novels, including *Patternmaster, Survivor* and *Parable of the Sower.*

— C —

Cameron, James is a civil rights activist, author and founder of the America's Black Holocaust Museum in Milwaukee. Cameron narrowly escaped lynching in 1930 by a Marion, Indiana, mob. His autobiography is *A Time of Terror.*

Campbell, Bebe Moore is a journalist who has written for the *New York Times*, the *Washington Post, Essence* and other publications. She is also a commentator on National Public Radio's *Morning Edition*, and the author of *Singing in the Comeback Choir* and *Your Blues Ain't Like Mine.*

Carney, Judith A. is a historical geographer, a professor at UCLA and the author of *Black Rice: The African Origins of Rice Cultivation in the Americas.*

Carson, Ben is director of pediatric neurosurgery at the Johns Hopkins Medical Institution in Baltimore, Maryland. He is world renowned for leading a medical team that separated West German conjoined twins in 1987. He is the author of *Gifted Hands, Think Big* and *The Big Picture.*

Carson, Clayborne is a professor of History and director of the Martin Luther King Jr. Papers Project at Stanford University. He edited the four-volume set, *The Papers of Martin Luther King, Jr.* and wrote *Malcolm X: The FBI Files*, as well as other writings.

Carter, Stephen L. has been a law professor at Yale University for twenty years, has published many works of nonfiction, including *Reflections of an Affirmative Action Baby*, *The Confirmation Mess: Cleaning Up the Federal Appointments Process*, *The Dissent of the Governed*, *Integrity*, and *Civility: Manners, Morals, and the Etiquette of Democracy*. His first work of fiction is *The Emperor of Ocean Park*.

Cary, Lorene is the author of *Black Ice*, her memoir, and *The Price of a Child*, a work of fiction.

Chafe, William Henry is a Duke University historian and editor of *Remembering Jim Crow: African Americans Tell About Life in the Segregated South*.

Chestnutt, Charles W. (1858–1932) was a lawyer and author known for writing short stories. Some of his writings include *The Goophered Grapevine*, *The Conjure Woman and Other Conjure Tales* and *The House Behind the Cedars*.

Clarke, John Henrik (1915–1998) was a historian and writer of more than two hundred short stories and producer of well over forty major historical and literary documents, including *African People at the Crossroads*. He also coedited *Africa, Lost and Found* (with Richard Moore and Keith Baird), *William Styron's Nat Turner: Ten Black Writers Respond*.

Cleage, Pearl is a playwright, performer and author of *What Looks Like Crazy on an Ordinary Day*, *I Wish I Had a Red Dress* and *Some Things I Never Thought I'd Do*.

Cleaver, Eldridge (1935–1998) was a writer, social activist and Black Panther Party leader in the 1960s. He is most noted for his autobiography, *Soul on Ice*. He later wrote *Soul on Fire*.

Clegg, Claude Andrew, III is a professor of History at Indiana University and the author of *An Original Man: The Life and Times of Elijah Muhammad*.

Cogan, Jim has worked for fifteen years as a recording engineer and producer who has helped to create some of the most critically acclaimed albums in jazz of the past twenty years. He coauthored (with award-winning author and playwright William Clark) *Temples of Sound: Inside the Great Recording Studios*.

Collier-Thomas, Bettye is a professor of History and director of the Center for African American History and Culture at Temple University. She is the author of *Daughters of Thunder: Black Women Preachers and Their Sermons 1850–1979*, and coauthor (with V. P. Franklin) *My Soul Is a Witness: A Chronology of the Civil Rights Era, 1954–1965*.

Collins, Lisa Gail is an assistant professor of Art History at Vassar College. She is coeditor of *African American Artists, 1929–1945: Prints, Drawings, and Paintings in The Metropolitan Museum of Art*.

Cooper, J. California is a playwright and author of numerous short story collections, including *A Piece of Mine, Homemade Love* and *Some Soul to Keep*.

Cottman, Michael H. is a prizewinning journalist for the *Washington Post* and an avid scuba diver. His books include *Spirit Dive: An African-American's Journey to Uncover a Sunken Slave Ship's Past* and a book of photography (coedited with Deborah Willis), *The Million Man March*.

Crafts, Hannah (1800s) is said to be the first African American slave woman to write a novel, *The Bondwoman's Narrative*. All that is known about Hannah Crafts has been gleaned through her writing.

Crews, Donald is a freelance artist, photographer and designer who has written and illustrated many books for young children. His most famous works include *Truck* and *Freight Train*. He has published more than twenty picture books.

— D —

Danticat, Edwidge is a Haitian-born novelist who has written several novels, including *Krik? Krak!, Breath, Eyes, Memory* and *The Farming of Bones*.

Davis, Ossie is a writer, actor, director and is married to actress Ruby Dee. He is the author of the critically acclaimed play *Purlie Victorious* and coauthor (with Ruby Dee) of *With Ossie and Ruby: In This Life Together*, a memoir.

Dee, Ruby is a stage, film and TV actress. She is married to Ossie Davis. Ruby Dee's acting career has spanned more than fifty years. *With Ossie and Ruby: In This Life Together* is their memoir.

Delany, Martin R. (1812–1885) was a doctor, civil rights activist and scholar. He was the first black field officer in the U.S. Army and is author of several books and essays including *Blake: Or the Huts of America* and *The Origin of Race and Color*.

Diakite, Baba Wague is a West African storyteller, painter, sculptor and ceramic artist. He is the author of *The Hunterman and the Crocodile* and *The Hatseller and the Monkeys*.

D'Orso, Michael is a journalist and author of *Like Judgment Day: The Ruin and Redemption of a Town Called Rosewood* and has collaborated on many notable titles, including *Walking with the Wind: A Memoir of Movement*, with Senator John Lewis.

Dove, Rita was poet laureate of the United States from 1993 to 1995. Her publications include the novel *Through the Ivory Gate*, a collection of stories, a verse drama, a book of essays and five books of poetry, among them *Thomas and Beulah*, which was awarded the Pulitzer Prize in 1987. She is Commonwealth Professor of English at the University of Virginia.

Dray, Philip is a writer and historian. He is the author of *At the Hands of Persons Unknown: The Lynching of Black America* and the coauthor (with Seth Cagin) of *We Are Not Afraid: The Story of Goodman, Schwerner, and Chaney and the Civil Rights Campaign for Mississippi*.

Driskell, David C. is a professor of Art at the University of Maryland, College Park, and one of the world's leading authorities on African American Art, as well as a commissioner of the Smithsonian's National Museum of African Art and the Amistad Research Center. He is the author of several exhibition books, including *Hidden Heritage: African American Art 1800–1950*, *Harlem Renaissance: Art of Black America* and *Contemporary Visual Expressions*.

Du Bois, W.E.B. (1868–1963) was a gifted intellectual, scholar, author and pioneering Pan-Africanist. His legacy of major writings includes *The Philadelphia Negro, Souls of Black Folk* and *Black Reconstruction in America, 1860–1880*.

Due, Tananarive is an award-winning author. Her books include *The Between, The Black Rose, My Soul to Keep* and *The Living Blood*.

Dunbar, Paul Laurence (1872–1906) was the first African American to gain national prominence as a poet. He was prolific, writing short stories, novels, librettos, plays, songs and essays as well as the poetry for which he became well known. His works include a self-published collection called *Oak and Ivy, Majors and Minors, Lyrics of Lowly Life, Lyrics of the Hearthside* and *Lyrics of Love and Laughter.*

Dunham, Katherine is an anthropologist, dancer, choreographer and the author of *Island Possessed.* She is best known for her choreography based on African American, Caribbean, West African and South American cultures.

Dunning, Jennifer is a *New York Times* dance critic and author of *Alvin Ailey: A Life in Dance* and *Geoffrey Holder: A Life in Theater, Dance, and Art.*

Dyson, Michael Eric is an Avalon Foundation Professor in the Humanities at the University of Pennsylvania. He has written several books, including *Reflecting Black: African-American Cultural Criticism, Race Rules: Navigating the Color Line* and *Open Mike: Reflections on Philosophy, Race, Sex, Culture and Religion.*

— E —

Elam, Harry J. is coeditor (with Robert Alexander) of *Colored Contradictions: An Anthology of Contemporary African-American Plays,* and the Christensen Professor for the Humanities, director of the Introduction to the Humanities, director of Graduate Studies for Drama, and director of the Committee on Black Performing Arts at Stanford University.

Ellison, Ralph (1914–1994) was the Albert Schweitzer Professor of the Humanities at New York University and lectured extensively on black folk culture. He achieved international fame for his first novel, *Invisible Man.*

Emery, Lynne Fauley is a dance historian and author of *Black Dance: From 1619 to Today.*

Entman, Robert is a professor of Communication at North Carolina State University and the coauthor (with Andrew Rojecki) of *The Black Image in the White Mind; Media and Race in America*. His forthcoming new book is *Living Black and White: Media and Race in America*.

Everett, Percival is a professor of English at the University of Southern California College of Letters, Arts and Sciences. He has written many books, including *Big Picture*, *Watershed*, *Erasure* and *God's Country*.

— F —

Fauset, Jessie Redmon (1882–1961) was a poet, novelist and an editor of *Crisis*, the magazine of NAACP. Fauset was one of the first female African American graduates of Cornell. Her books portray the experiences of African American women, including *Plum Bun: A Novel Without a Moral*, *There Is Confusion* and others.

Feelings, Muriel is an author of children's books, including *Zamani Goes to Market* and *Moja Means One: Swahili Counting Book*. She collaborated with author/illustrator Tom Feelings on *Jambo Means Hello: Swahili Alphabet Book*.

Feelings, Tom is a fine artist and illustrator of over twenty books, seven of them children's books. He is best known for the narrative drawings in his book *The Middle Passage*.

Files, Lolita is the author of *Child of God*, *Scenes from a Sistah* and *Getting to the Good Part*.

Fisher, Angela is an Australian photographer best known for her work featured in *Africa Adorned*. She coauthored (with Carol Beckwith) *African Ceremonies* and *Passages: Photographs in Africa*.

Flournoy, Valerie is a children's author who visits schools across the country, giving a show-and-tell program on how she turns her stories into books. She is the author of *The Best Time of Day*, *Twins Strike Back* and *The Patchwork Quilt*, which won the Christopher Medal, the Coretta Scott King Award and the Ezra Jack Keats Award.

Foner, Eric is the DeWitt Clinton Professor of History at Columbia University. He specializes in the Civil War and Reconstruction, slavery, and nineteenth-century America. He is the author of *Reconstruction: America's Unfinished Revolution, 1863–1877*, *The Story of American Freedom* and *Who Owns History?: Rethinking the Past in a Changing World*.

Fordham, John is a British jazz critic and broadcaster. He has written extensively on jazz for several international magazines. His books include *Jazz: History, Instruments, Musicians, Recordings* and *The Sound of Jazz: An Illustrated Jazz History*.

Forrest, Leon (1937–1997) was a professor and former department chair of African American studies at Northwestern University. He wrote *Divine Days* and *Relocations of the Spirit* as well as several other novels.

Foster, Frances Smith is a Charles Howard Candler Professor of English at Emory University. She has edited and coedited numerous books including *Incidents in the Life of a Slave Girl*; *Behind the Scenes*; *The Oxford Companion to African American Literature* and *Minnie's Sacrifice, Sowing and Reaping, Trial and Triumph: Three Rediscovered Novels*.

Franklin, John Hope is a writer and historian most known for *From Slavery to Freedom: A History of African Americans* (with Alfred A. Moss Jr.). He is the professor emeritus of History at Duke University. His most recent book, *My Life and an Era: The Autobiography of Buck Colbert Franklin*, is an autobiography of his father that he edited with his son, John Whittington Franklin.

Freeman, Roland has been a field research associate for the Smithsonian Institution for more than twenty years. He is president of the Group for Cultural Documentation based in Washington, D.C. He is the author of *A Communion of the Spirits: African American Quilters, Preservers, and Their Stories.*

French, Albert L. is a novelist who began writing to battle his way out of depression. His books include *Billy, Patches of Fire: A Story of War and Reconstruction* and *I Can't Wait on God.*

— G —

Gabbin, Joanne V. is a professor of English at James Madison University. She is the author of *Sterling A. Brown: Building the Black Aesthetic Tradition* and editor of *The Furious Flowering of African American Poetry.*

Gaines, Ernest J. is a professor and writer-in-residence at the University of Southwestern Louisiana in Lafayette. He is a fiction writer best known for *The Autobiography of Miss Jane Pittman* and *A Lesson Before Dying.*

Gates, Henry Louis, Jr. is an educator, scholar, literary critic and writer. He is chair of the Afro-American Studies Department at Harvard University, and has edited and written many books, including *The Classic Slave Narratives, The Norton Anthology of African American Literature* and *The Bondwoman's Narra-tive.*

George, Nelson writes on urban culture and is known for writing *The Death of Rhythm & Blues; Buppies, B-Boys, Baps and Bohos: Notes on Post-Soul Black Culture* and *Hip Hop America.*

Gilbert, Derrick I. M. (a.k.a. D-Knowledge) is the editor (with Tony Medina) of *Catch the Fire!!!: A Cross-Generational Anthology of Contemporary African-American Poetry* and author of *HennaMan,* a book of poetry.

Giovanni, Nikki is a world-renowned poet, writer, commentator, activist and educator. She is the University Distinguished Professor of English at Virginia Tech. Giovanni has written more than two dozen books, including volumes of poetry, illustrated children's books and three collections of essays. Her most recent volumes of poetry are *Love Poems, Blues: For All the Changes* and *Quilting the Black-Eyed Pen: Poems and Not Quite Poems.*

Goodwine, Marquetta L. is an environmental and cultural activist, author, playwright, lecturer and performer. She is the author of *The Legacy of Ibo Landing: Gullah Roots of African American Culture.*

Gray, Herman is a professor of Sociology at the University of California at Santa Cruz. He is the author of *Producing Jazz: The Experience of an Independent Record Company* and *Watching Race: Television and the Struggle for "Blackness."*

Greenfield, Eloise is a children's author who has been writing for more than thirty years. Her works include *I Make Music, On My Horse* and *Honey, I Love and Other Love Poems.*

Grifalconi, Ann is an award-winning illustrator of over fifty books for children. She has written and illustrated stories set in Africa, including *The Village of Round and Square Houses, Darkness and the Butterfly, Osa's Pride* and *Flyaway Girl.*

Griffin, Farah Jasmine is a Columbia University professor, Billie Holiday historian and author of *If You Can't Be Free, Be a Mystery: In Search of Billie Holiday.*

Grimes, Nikki is a poet, novelist, journalist and educator. She is an award-winning author of more than two dozen children's books, including *Meet Danitra Brown, My Man Blue* and *Bronx Masquerade.*

— H —

Hacker, Andrew is professor emeritus of Political Science at Queens College. He is the author of *Two Nations: Black and White, Separate, Hostile, Unequal*, *Money: Who Has How Much and Why* and *Mismatch: The Growing Gulf Between Men and Women*.

Haley, Alex (1921–1992) was an American biographer, scriptwriter and author who became famous with the publication of *Roots*. He cowrote (with Malcolm X) *The Autobiography of Malcolm X* in 1965.

Haley, Gail E. is a storyteller, puppeteer, artist and author of award-winning children's books. She wrote the children's classic and Caldecott Medal winner *A Story, A Story* and England's Kate Greenaway Medal award-winning *The Post Office Cat*. She has also coauthored other educational books and programs on Media Literacy.

Hall, Wade is professor emeritus of English and the Humanities at Bellarmine College. He is also the author of numerous books, including *Passing for Black: The Life and Careers of Mae Street Kidd* and *The Rest of the Dream: The Black Odyssey of Lyman Johnson*.

Hamilton, Virginia (1936–2002) was an acclaimed young adults' and children's author. Some of her works include *The People Could Fly: American Black Folktales*, *Sweet Whispers, Brother Rush* and *A Little Love*.

Hampton, Henry (1940–1998) was the founder and president of Blackside, Inc., the independent documentary film company best known for the PBS documentaries *Eyes on the Prize* and *Malcolm X: Make It Plain*. He coauthored *Voices of Freedom: An Oral History of America's Civil Rights Movement from the 1950s Through the 1980s*, the companion book to *Eyes on the Prize*.

Hansen, Joyce is the author of several books, including *Breaking Ground, Breaking Silence: The Story of New York's African Burial Ground* and *Gift-Giver and the Captive*.

Harding, Vincent is a professor of Religion and Social Transformation at the Iliff School of Theology. His works include *There Is a River: The Black Struggle for Freedom in America, Hope and History: Why We Must Share the Story of the Movement* and *Martin Luther King: The Inconvenient Hero*.

Harms, Robert is a professor of History at Yale University. He is the author of *The Diligent: A Voyage Through the Worlds of the Slave Trade* and *River of Wealth, River of Sorrow: The Central Zaire Basin in the Era of the Slave and Ivory Trade, 1500–1891*.

Harper, Frances E. W. (1825–1911) is the best-known African American writer and poet of the nineteenth century. She wrote *Minnie's Sacrifice, Sowing and Reaping; Trial and Triumph: Three Rediscovered Novels* and *Iola Leroy; or, Shadows Uplifted*.

Harper, Michael S. is a poet and author of many collections of poems, two of which, *Dear John, Dear Coltrane* and *Images of Kin*, have been nominated for the National Book Award. He is coeditor of a critically acclaimed anthology, *Chant of Saints*, and is responsible for bringing poet Sterling A. Brown's *Collected Poems* into print.

Harris, Erich Leon (1965–2000) was an actor, writer and author of *African-American Screenwriters Now: Conversations with Hollywood's Black Pack*. He also appeared in plays, films, commercials and the *Power Rangers*.

Hatch, James V. is the coeditor (with Ted Shire) of the two-volume set *Black Theatre USA: Plays by African Americans*, and a leading historian and scholar in the area of theater, as well as a curator of one of the world's largest collections of black drama.

Haygood, Wil is a staff member of the *Washington Post*. He is the author of *King of the Cats: The Life and Times of Adam Clayton Powell, Jr.*, *Two on the River* and *The Haygoods of Columbus: A Family Memoir*.

Hayre, Ruth Wright (1910–1998) was an educator, school administrator and philanthropist. She is the author (with Alexis Moore) of *Tell Them We Are Rising: A Memoir of Faith in Education* and founder of the Tell Them We Are Rising scholarship foundation in Philadelphia.

Herron, Carolivia is a former professor of English and author of children's and adult fiction and a scholar in the field of classical epic and African American literature. Her books include the controversial children's book, *Nappy Hair*.

Higginson, Thomas Wentworth (1823–1911) was a Unitarian minister, abolitionist, poet and writer. He is the author of *Black Rebellion: Five Slave Revolts*, *Army Life in a Black Regiment* and other writings.

Hill, Donna is a public relations associate for the Queens Borough Public Library system. She is the author of many novels, including *Indiscretions*, *Rhythms* and *An Ordinary Woman*.

Hill, Robert A. is an associate professor of History at UCLA and director of the Marcus Garvey and Universal Improvement Association Papers Project of the African Studies Center. He is the editor of *Marcus Garvey, Life and Lessons: A Centennial Companion to the Marcus Garvey and Universal Negro Improvement Association Papers*.

Hilliard, David is the former chief of staff for the Black Panther Party and current executive director of the Dr. Huey P. Newton Foundation. Hilliard is the author (with Lewis Cole) of *This Side of Glory: The Autobiography of David Hilliard and the History of the Black Panther Party*.

Himes, Chester (1909–1984) was the author of nine detective novels and an expatriate who lived in France and Spain. *A Rage in Harlem*, *If He Hollers Let Him Go*, *Cast the First Stone* and *The Third Generation* are among his published works.

Hinton, Richard J. (1830–1901) was an abolitionist and commander of the First Kansas (colored) Infantry during the Civil War. He is the author of *John Brown and His Men.*

Hoffman, Mary is a children's author who has published over eighty books. Her book *Stravaganza: City of Masks* is on the New York Public Library's 2003 Books for the Teen Age list. She is best known for her children's books *Amazing Grace* and *Boundless Grace*.

Hopkinson, Deborah is director of Grants and Advancement Services for Whitman College and the author of many children's books, including *Sweet Clara and the Freedom Quilt*, the companion book *Under the Quilt of Night* and *A Band of Angels*.

Horne, Gerald is a History professor at the University of North Carolina at Chapel Hill. Horne's recent publications include *Fire This Time: The Watts Uprising and the 1960s* and *Race Woman: The Lives of Shirley Graham Du Bois*.

Hort, Lenny is a children's author whose books include *How Many Stars in the Sky?*, *Goatherd and the Shepherdess* and *The Boy Who Held Back the Sea*.

Howard, Elizabeth Fitzgerald is a writer of children's literature. Her books include *Virgie Goes to School with Us Boys*, *Aunt Flossie's Hats (and Crab Cakes Later)* and *What's in Aunt Mary's Room?*

Hughes, Langston (1902–1967) was a prolific poet, novelist, editor, lecturer and playwright. He achieved fame as a poet during the Harlem Renaissance. His long and distinguished career produced volumes of diverse genres and inspired the work of countless other African American writers. *Not Without Laughter* was his first novel.

Hudson, Cheryl Willis is vice president and editorial director of Just Us Books. She is also the author of numerous children's books. Some of her best-known books are *Afro Bets 123*, *Afro-Bets ABC* and *Bright Eyes, Brown Skin*.

Hurston, Zora Neale (1891–1960) was a novelist, folklorist and anthropologist best known for her powerful novel *Their Eyes Were Watching God*. Other novels by Hurston include *Moses, Man of the Mountain* and *Dust Tracks on a Road: An Autobiography*.

— I —

Irons, Peter H. is an award-winning historian and professor at the University of California, San Diego. He is the author of *May It Please the Court: Courts, Kids, and the Constitution* and *A People's History of the Supreme Court* (with Howard Zinn).

— J —

Jackson-Opoku, Sandra is a poet and author best known for *The River Where Blood Is Born* and *Hot Johnny (and the Women Who Loved Him)*.

Johnson, Angela is a poet, novelist and writer of children's books. She won the Coretta Scott King Author Award for several of her books, including *When I Am Old With You*. She wrote *Heaven, the Other Side: Shorter Poems* and *Toning the Sweep*.

Johnson, Charles is an author, novelist and essayist who wrote *King: The Photobiography of Martin Luther King, Jr.* (with Bob Adleman) and *Middle Passage*.

Johnson, James Weldon (1871–1938) was a songwriter, poet, novelist, journalist, critic and autobiographer. He and his brother, Rosamond, cowrote *Lift Every Voice and Sing*, the Negro National Anthem. His other books include *The Autobiography of an Ex-colored Man* and *The Book of American Negro Poetry*.

Johnson, Walter A. is an associate professor of History at New York University and the author of *Soul by Soul: Life Inside the Antebellum Slave Market*.

Jones, G. William (d. 1993) was a professor of Cinema and Video at Southern Methodist University. He started the G. William Jones Film and Video Collection, originally called the Southwest Film/Video Archives, in 1970. He is known for writing *Black Cinema Treasures: Lost and Found*.

Jones, James H. is a professor of History at the University of Arkansas and the author of *Bad Blood: The Tuskegee Syphilis Experiment*.

Jordan, June (1936–2002) was a poet, novelist, essayist and political activist. She authored many books and is noted for her memoir *Soldier: A Poet's Childhood* and other books, including her first novel, *His Own Where*, and her books of essays *Technical Difficulties: African American Notes on the State of the Union* and *Some of Us Did Not Die: New and Selected Essays of June Jordan*.

— K —

Keats, Ezra Jack (1916–1983) is known for his award-winning children's books with their collage and paint illustrations, particularly *The Snowy Day*, and six other books featuring the character Peter, including *Whistle for Willie*, *Peter's Chair*, *A Letter to Amy*, *Goggles!*, *Hi Cat!* and *Pet Show!*. He authored over eighty-five children's books.

Kenan, Randall is a journalist and author who has written for the *Nation, Spin,* the *New York Times Book Review, Callaloo* and *Emerge.* His first book of fiction was *A Visitation of Spirits.* He also wrote *Let the Dead Bury Their Dead,* a collection of short stories and *Walking on Water: Black American Lives at the Turn of the Twenty-first Century.*

Kidd, Mae Street (1904–1999) was a Kentucky state representative for seventeen years. Her memoir is *Passing for Black: The Life and Careers of Mae Street Kidd.*

Kincaid, Jamaica is a novelist from Antigua. Kincaid addresses several major themes in her writing that include the influence of homeland on identity and culture, the desire for independence and female bonding. Her writings include *Annie John, The Autobiography of My Mother* and *At the Bottom of the River.*

King, Martin Luther, Jr. (1929–1968) was a Baptist minister, civil rights leader and Nobel Peace Prize winner known for his philosophy of nonviolent direct action. He wrote numerous books and speeches, including *I've Been to the Mountaintop, Letter from Birmingham Jail* and *Why We Can't Wait.*

King, Woodie, Jr. is a producer and director who established the New Federal Theatre in 1970. He is the author of *The Impact of Race: Theatre and Culture, The National Black Drama Anthology: Eleven Plays from America's Leading African-American Theaters* and *New Plays for the Black Theatre.*

Kloss, Jethro (1863–1946) pioneered the ideas that led to the flourishing of the natural-foods industry. He is the author of several natural-health books and is best known for *Back to Eden.*

Kroll, Virginia has written more than twenty picture books, including *Masai and I, Fireflies, Peach Pies & Lullabies, Africa Brothers and Sisters* and *Wood-hoopoe Willie.*

— L —

Larsen, Nella (1891–1964) was an author and novelist of the Harlem Renaissance. She wrote *The Wrong Man*, *Quicksand* and *Passing*.

Lemann, Nicholas is a staff writer for the *New York Times*. He has written several books, including *The Promised Land: The Great Black Migration and How It Changed America* and *The Big Test: The Secret History of the American Meritocracy*.

Lester, Julius is a writer of children's literature. Lester has published twenty-five books. His works include *Sam and the Tigers*, *Long Journey Home* and *To Be a Slave*.

Lewis, David Levering is professor of History at Rutgers University and author of the Pulitzer Prize–winning *W.E.B. DuBois: Biography of a Race 1868–1919*. He also edited *The Portable Harlem Renaissance Reader*.

Lewis, John is a congressman from Georgia and civil rights activist. He cowrote (with Michael D'Orso) *Walking with the Wind: A Memoir of the Movement*.

Lewis, Samella is professor emeritus of Art History at Scripps College and an internationally renowned artist, author, filmmaker and art advocate. She is the founding editor of the *International Review of African American Art* and the founding director of the Museum of African American Art in Los Angeles. She wrote *African American Art and Artists*.

Licks, Dr. (**Allan Slutsky**) is a music producer and arranger. He is one of the pioneers of guitar tab and note-for-note transcriptions. He is the author of *Standing in the Shadows of Motown: The Life and Music of Legendary Bassist James Jamerson*.

Light, Alan is a founding editor of *Vibe* magazine and editor of *The VIBE History of Hip Hop*.

Litwak, Leon F. is a Pulitzer Prize–winning historian, writer and professor at the University of California. His notable works include *Trouble in Mind: Black Southerners in the Age of Jim Crow* and *Been in the Storm So Long: The Aftermath of Slavery*.

Lorde, Audre (1934–1992) was a critically acclaimed novelist, poet and essayist. Her first prose collection, *The Cancer Journals*, won the American Library Association Gay Caucus Book of the Year for 1981. Her works include *Undersong: Chosen Poems Old and New*, *Our Dead Behind Us* and *Zami: A New Spelling of My Name*.

— **M** —

Madigan, Tim is an author and journalist. His books include *The Burning: Massacre, Destruction, and the Tulsa Race Riot of 1921*.

Madison, James H. is a History professor at Indiana University and author of *A Lynching in the Heartland: Race and Memory in America*.

Marable, Manning is a historian and director of the Institute for Research in African-American Studies at Columbia University. His many books include *The Great Wells of Democracy: The Meaning of Race in American Life* and *Freedom: A Photographic History of the African American Struggle*. He is also coeditor (with Leith Mullings) of *Let Nobody Turn Us Around*.

Marshall, Paule has taught at Yale, Columbia, Cornell and Oxford Universities, and has won numerous prizes and awards. She has written several novels, including *Praisesong for the Widow*, *The Chosen Place* and *The Timeless People*.

Mason, John is a Yoruba priest and an author who has written numerous books on Yoruba religion and culture. He has traveled extensively in Cuba and Nigeria. His writings include *Black Gods: Orisa Studies in the New World* and *Four New World Yoruba Rituals*.

Massood, Paula J. is an associate professor in the film department of Brooklyn College/CUNY. She is the author of *Black City Cinema: African American Urban Experiences in Film*.

Mathis, Sharon Bell is a children's author, librarian at the Patricia Roberts Harris Educational Center and a founding member of the children's literature division of the Washington, D.C., Black Writers' Workshop. Her books include *The Hundred Penny Box* and *Teacup Full of Roses*.

McDermott, Gerald is a children's author, illustrator and filmmaker. He has written several books, including *Anansi the Spider: A Tale from the Ashanti* and *Zomo the Rabbit: A Trickster Tale from West Africa*.

McFadden, Bernice L. is author of the national best-sellers *Sugar*, *The Warmest December*, *This Bitter Earth* and *Loving Donovan*, her most recent novel.

McGill, Alice is a children's author best known for her book *In the Hollow of Your Hand: Slave Lullabies*.

McKay, Claude (1889–1948) was a poet and novelist born in Jamaica. He was the first black best-selling author, with *Home to Harlem*. His lesser-known works include *Banana Bottom* and his memoir, *A Long Way from Home*.

McKinney-Whetstone, Diane is the author of the national best-selling novel *Tumbling*, and the widely acclaimed follow-up, *Tempest Rising*. Her third novel is *Blues Dancing*.

McKissack, Patricia is a children's author who often collaborates with her husband, Frederick. Her books include *Flossie and the Fox*, *A Long Hard Journey: The Story of the Pullman Porter* and *Sojourner Truth: Ain't I a Woman?*

McMillan, Terry is a novelist who became famous with her *New York Times* best-seller *Waiting to Exhale*. She also wrote *Mama* and *How Stella Got Her Groove Back* and edited *Breaking Ice: An Anthology of Contemporary African-American Fiction*.

McPherson, James M. is George Henry Davis Professor of American History at Princeton University. He wrote several historical books including *Crossroads of Freedom* and *Battle Cry of Freedom: The Civil War Era*.

Mendez, Phil is an award-winning children's author best known for *The Black Snowman*.

Merlis, Bob is a former vice president at Warner Music. He coauthored (with Davin Seary) *Heart and Soul: A Celebration of Black Music Style in America 1930–1975*.

Messinger, Lisa Mintz is an associate curator in the department of modern art at The Metropolitan Museum of Art and coeditor of *African American Artists, 1929–1945: Prints, Drawings, and Paintings in The Metropolitan Museum of Art*.

Metress, Christopher is an associate professor of English at Samford University and author of *The Lynching of Emmett Till: A Documentary Narrative*.

Mills, Kay is a former editorial writer for the *Los Angeles Times* and the author of *This Little Light of Mine: The Life of Fannie Lou Hamer* and *Place in the News: From the Women's Pages to the Front Page*.

Mitchell, Margaree King is a dramatist, playwright and author best known for her children's books *Uncle Jed's Barbershop* and *Granddaddy's Gift*.

Mollel, Tololwa M. is a Tanzanian storyteller who uses traditional folklore as the basis for his popular storybooks. He is the author of *The Orphan Boy*, *Kele's Secret*, *A Promise to the Sun: An African Story* and *Rhino's Boy: A Maasai Legend*.

Morrison, Toni is the Robert F. Goheen Professor in the Council of the Humanities at Princeton University. Her seven major novels, *The Bluest Eye*, *Sula*, *Song of Solomon*, *Tar Baby*, *Beloved*, *Jazz* and *Paradise*, have received extensive critical acclaim. She won the Pulitzer Prize in 1988 for her novel *Beloved*, and the National Book Critics Award in 1977 for *Song of Solomon*. In 1993, Morrison was the first African American winner of the Nobel Prize and the first woman to win since 1938.

Mosley, Walter is a professor of English at New York University and the author of the best-selling Easy Rawlins mystery series, including *Devil in a Blue Dress*, *A Red Death* and the most recent, *Six Easy Pieces*. He is also the author of several science fiction novels, including *Blue Light* and *Futureland*.

Mullings, Leith is presidential professor in the Ph.D. program in Anthropology at the CUNY Graduate Center. She coedited (with Manning Marable) *Let Nobody Turn Us Around: An Anthology of African American Social and Political Thought from Slavery to the Present* and *Freedom*. She is also the author of *On Our Own Terms: Race, Class and Gender in the Lives of African American Women*.

Musgrove, Margaret W. lived in Ghana where she did extensive research for her children's book *Ashanti to Zulu: African Traditions*.

Myers, Walter Dean is a novelist who has been writing for more than thirty years. His works include *One More River to Cross:*

An African American Photograph Album, Scorpions and *Now Is Your Time!: The African American Struggle forFreedom.*

— N —

Naylor, Gloria is the author of several books, including *The Women of Brewster Place*, *Linden Hills*, *Mama Day* and *Bailey's Cafe*. In addition to her novels, she has written essays and screenplays, as well as the stage adaptation of *Bailey's Cafe*.

Nelson, Angela M. S. is an assistant professor of Popular Culture at Bowling Green State University and director of its Center for Popular Culture Studies. She edited *This Is How We Flow: Rhythm in Black Cultures* and is a contributor to *Cultural Diversity and the U.S. Media.*

Nelson, Jill is a freelance writer and author of *Police Brutality: An Anthology*, *Volunteer Slavery: My Authentic Negro Experience*, *Straight Up*, *No Chaser* and *Sexual Healing.*

Newman, Richard is the research officer for the W.E.B. Du Bois Institute for Afro-American Research at Harvard University and author of *Go Down Moses: Celebrating the African-American Spiritual.*

Newton, Huey P. (1942–1989) was cofounder of the Black Panther Party and symbol of Black urban resistance. He wrote *War Against the Panthers: A Study of Repression in America.*

— O —

Olson, Lynne is a journalist and author best known for *Freedom's Daughters: The Unsung Heroines of the Civil Rights Movement from 1830 to 1970.*

Onyefulu, Ifeoma is a photographer and author of children's books. She was brought up in a traditional Nigerian village in eastern Nigeria. Onyefulu and her children travel back to Africa and walk from village to village, talking with people they meet and waiting to find just the right photograph. She is the author of *A Is for Africa, Emeka's Gift: An African Counting Story* and *Ebele's Favourite: A Book of African Games*.

Owens, William A. is a folklorist, educator and author of *Black Mutiny* and other books, as well as articles, reviews and short stories.

— P —

Packard, Jerrold M. is a historian and author of many books, including *American Nightmare: The History of Jim Crow*.

Painter, Nell Irvin is a writer, scholar and historian. Her books include *Sojourner Truth: A Life, a Symbol* and *Southern History Across the Color Line*.

Parks, Gordon, Jr. is an award-winning photographer, writer, filmmaker, composer and musician. He directed *The Learning Tree*, which was an adaptation of his autobiography by the same name, and is the author of *A Choice of Weapons*, another memoir.

Petry, Ann (1908–1997) was the author of *The Street*, the first novel by an African American woman to sell more than one million copies. She also wrote *Miss Muriel and Other Stories* and *The Narrows*.

Pinkney, Andrea Davis is head of Houghton Mifflin's children's division and author of *Ella Fitzgerald: The Tale of a Vocal Virtuosa* and *Let It Shine: Stories of Black Women Freedom Fighters*.

Pinkney, Brian is a visual artist, writer and illustrator of many children's books, including *Max Found Two Sticks, Jojo's Flying Side Kick, The Adventures of Sparrowboy* and *Cosmo and the Robot*.

Pinkney, Gloria Jean is a writer of children's books. Her first book was *Back Home* followed by the prequel *Sunday Outing.*

Pollitzer, William S. is professor emeritus of Anatomy and Anthropology at the University of North Carolina at Chapel Hill. He is the author of *The Gullah People and Their African Heritage.*

Porter, Kenneth W. is the author of *The Black Seminoles: History of a Freedom-Seeking People.*

Powell, Richard J. is John Spencer Bassett Professor of Art and Art History at Duke University. He is the author of *Black Art: A Cultural History* and coauthor (with Jock Reynolds) of *To Conserve a Legacy: American Art from Historically Black Colleges and Universities.*

Price, Leontyne is a famous black opera singer who has won over twenty Grammy Awards. A graduate of the Juilliard School of Music, Price performed in 118 operas between 1961 and 1969. She is the author of the children's book *Aida.*

Price, Richard is an anthropologist and the author of *Maroon Societies: Rebel Slave Communities in the Americas.*

— **R** —

Rampersad, Arnold is Sara Hart Kimball Professor in the Humanities at Stanford University. He is the author or editor of many books and essays on Langston Hughes, Richard Wright, Ralph Ellison and W.E.B. Du Bois.

Reed, Ishmael is one of the most reviewed and controversial writers in America. He is the author of numerous books, including *The Freelance Pallbearers, Yellow Back Radio Broke-Down* and *Shrovetide in New Orleans.*

Rhodes, Jewell Parker is a professor of Creative Writing and American Literature at Arizona State University. Her stories have been anthologized in *Children of the Night: Best Short Stories by Black Writers 1967 to the Present* and *Ancestral House: The Black Short Story in the Americas and Europe.*

Rickford, John Russell is a professor of Linguistics at Stanford University and an authority on Ebonics. Rickford cowrote (with his son Russell Rickford) *Spoken Soul: The Story of Black English.*

Ridley, John is a film and television producer and an author. He has written several novels, including *A Conversation with the Mann, Those Who Walk in Darkness* and *The Drift.* His novel *Stray Dogs* was made into the movie *U-Turn.* He wrote and produced the film *Undercover Brother,* conceived the story for the film *Three Kings* and also wrote and directed *Cold Around the Heart.*

Ringgold, Faith is a professor of Art at the University of California in San Diego and the author of many books, including *Tar Beach, The Invisible Princess* and *Cassie's Word Quilt.* She is best known for her painted story quilts and has illustrated eleven children's books.

Roberts, John W. is the editor of *From Hucklebuck to Hip Hop: Social Dance in the African-American Community in Philadelphia.* He is head of the Afro-American Studies Department and associate professor of Folklore and Folk Life at the University of Pennsylvania.

Robertson, David is a film consultant and author of *Denmark Vesey: The Buried Story of America's Largest Slave Rebellion and the Man Who Led It, Booth: A Novel* and *Sly and Able: A Political Biography of James F. Byrnes.*

Ross, Lawrence C., Jr. is the author of *The Divine Nine: The History of African American Fraternities and Sororities* and *The Ways of Black Folks: A Year in the Life of a People.*

Rowan, Carl T. (1925–2000) was an African American federal cabinet member, international ambassador and nationally known syndicated newspaper columnist, once called "America's most visible black journalist." He is the author of *Dream Makers, Dream Breakers: The World of Justice Thurgood Marshall*.

— S —

Sampson, Henry T. is a film historian and the author of *Blacks in Black and White: A Source Book on Black Films*.

San Souci, Robert D. has written over eighty-three children's books, collaborating on nine of them, including *The Hired Hand: An African American Tale*, *The Twins and the Bird of Darkness: A Hero Tale from the Caribbean* and *The Secret of the Stone* with his brother, Daniel San Souci, who is an illustrator and author.

Savio, Joanne is a photographer known for her collection of portraits in *Vital Grace: The Black Male Dancer*.

Seeger, Pete is a Grammy Award–winning folk singer and American legend. He has written several books, including such children's books as *Abiyoyo* and (with Paul DuBois Jacobs) *Pete Seeger's Storytelling Book*.

Séjour, Victor (1817–1874) was a Louisiana-born playwright who immigrated to Paris before the age of twenty. He wrote "The Mulatto," a short story.

Shakur, Assata is a former Black Panther and Black Liberation Army leader during the 1970s. She escaped from prison and was given political asylum in Cuba, where she has lived since 1986. *Assata* is her memoir.

Sinnette, Elinor Des Verney is an oral historian and biographer. She is the author of *Arthur Alfonso Schomburg: Black Bibliophile and Collector.*

Smith, Jessie Carney is Camille and William Cosby professor in the Humanities and university librarian at Fisk University. She is a noted editor of *Notable Black American Women* and *Notable Black American Men.*

Smith, Suzanne E. is an associate professor of U.S. History at George Mason University. She is the author of *Dancing in the Street: Motown and the Cultural Politics of Detroit*, and has contributed to various public history projects, including Rachel Carson's film *Silent Spring* for PBS, and the series *I'll Make Me a World: African American Arts in the Twentieth Century* for Blackside Productions.

Snead, James (d. 1989) was the author of *White Screens, Black Images: Hollywood from the Dark Side.*

Southern, Eileen (1920–2002) became Harvard's first black female tenured professor in 1976. An expert on Renaissance and African American music, she is the author of *The Music of Black Americans: A History.*

Stauffer, John is an associate professor of English and American Civilization at Harvard University. His most recent works include *The Black Hearts of Men: Radical Abolitionists and the Transformation of Race* and *John Brown and the Coming of the Civil War.*

Steptoe, John (1950–1989) was the author and illustrator of many books, including *The Story of Jumping Mouse* and *Mufaro's Beautiful Daughters: An African Tale,* both of which received the Caldecott Honor Medal.

Stewart, James Brewer is the James Wallace Professor of History at Macalaster College and author of *Holy Warriors: The*

Abolitionists and American Slavery and *Blind Eye: The Terrifying Story of a Doctor Who Got Away with Murder*.

Story, Rosalyn is a violinist with the Fort Worth Symphony and a leading authority on African Americans in classical music in America. She is the author of *And So I Sing: African American Divas of Opera and Concert*.

Styron, William is an award-winning novelist and political activist who has written numerous books, including the controversial *The Confessions of Nat Turner*, *Sophie's Choice* and *Shadrach*, both of which have been made into feature-length films.

— T —

Tademy, Lalita is a former vice president at Sun Microsystems and the author of the historical novel *Cane River*.

Tate, Eleanora E. is an award-winning children's book author whose books include *African American Musicians* and *The Secret of Gumbo Grove*.

Taulbert, Clifton L. is an author and lecturer best known for his memoir *Once Upon a Time When We Were Colored*. He also wrote *The Last Train North*, *Watching Our Crops Come In*, *Eight Habits of the Heart* and the children's picture book *Little Cliff and the Porch People*.

Taylor, Yuval is an editor at Lawrence Hill Books best known for editing *I Was Born a Slave: An Anthology of Classic Slave Narratives, Volume Two 1849–1866* and *The Future of Jazz*.

Temple-Raston, Dina is a journalist and author of *A Death in Texas: A Story of Race, Murder, and a Small Town's Struggle for Redemption*.

Thomas, Hugh is the author of *The Slave Trade: The Story of the Atlantic Slave Trade: 1440–1870*.

Thomas, Velma Maia is an author, historian and genealogist. She is the creator of the Black Holocaust Exhibit at the Shrine of the Black Madonna Bookstore in Atlanta, Georgia. Her interactive books include *Lest We Forget: The Passage from Africa to Slavery and Emancipation*, *Freedom's Children: The Passage from Emancipation to the Great Migration* and *We Shall Not Be Moved: The Passage from the Great Migration to the Million Man March*.

Thompson, Kathleen was the editor-in-chief for the *Encyclopedia of Black Women* and coeditor (with Darlene Clark Hine) of *A Shining Thread of Hope: The History of Black Women in America*. She is the editor of *The Face of Our Past: Images of Black Women from Colonial America to the Present* (with Hilary MacAustin, photographic researcher).

Tobin, Jacqueline is a teacher, collector and author of *Hidden in Plain View: A Secret Story of Quilts and the Underground Railroad*.

Toomer, Jean (1894–1967) was a writer of poetry, fiction, essays and reviews. He is best known for *Cane*, written during the Harlem Renaissance.

Ture, Kwame (1941–1998) was a civil rights leader who first voiced the phrase "black power" in the mid-1960s. He is the coauthor (with Charles V. Hamilton) of *Black Power: The Politics of Liberation in America*.

Turner, Patricia A. is a professor of African American Studies at the University of California. Her books include *I Heard It Through the Grapevine: Rumor in African-American Culture* and *Ceramic Uncles and Celluloid Mammies: Black Images and Their Influence on Culture*.

— V —

Van Deburg, William L. is a historian of the African American experience who teaches classes on antebellum southern slavery and contemporary black popular culture. His books include *New Day in Babylon: The Black Power Movement and American Culture, 1965–1975* and *Black Camelot: African-American Culture Heroes in their Times, 1960–1980*.

Van Sertima, Ivan is a literary critic, linguist, anthropologist and writer. In 1977 he wrote *They Came Before Columbus: The African Presence in Ancient America*, now in its twenty-first printing. He has edited several major anthologies, including *Blacks in Science: Ancient and Modern, Black Women in Antiquity, Egypt Revisited* and *Nile Valley Civilizations*.

Vincent, Rickey teaches a Black Studies course, Black Protest Music 1965–1990s: Funk, Rap and the Black Revolution, at San Francisco University. He is the author of *Funk: The Music, the People, and the Rhythm of the One*.

Vorenburg, Michael is an assistant professor of History at Brown University and the author of *Final Freedom: The Civil War, the Abolition of Slavery, and the Thirteenth Amendment*.

— W—

Walker, Alice is a feminist, author and poet best known for her novel *The Color Purple*. Her numerous works include *The Third Life of Grange Copeland, Meridian, Possessing the Secret of Joy, Revolutionary Petunias* and *The Way Forward Is with a Broken Heart*.

Walker, David (1785–1830) was a free black born in Wilmington, North Carolina, who wrote one of America's most provocative political documents of the nineteenth century, *David Walker's Appeal to the Coloured Citizens of the World*.

Walker, Marcellus A. is the medical director of the Wayne Woodland Manor in Pennsylvania and founder of a multidisciplinary group practice in New Windsor, New York. He wrote (with Kenneth B. Singleton, M.D.) *Natural Health for African Americans: The Physicians' Guide.*

Walker, Margaret (1915–1998) was a poet and writer whose work spans more than four decades. She was known for her volumes of poetry, including *For My People, Prophets for a New Day* and *October Journey*. Her most famous work of fiction is *Jubilee*.

Walker, Persia is a former journalist and editor. Her first novel is *Harlem Redux*.

Walton, Anthony is writer-in-residence at Bowdoin College. He is the author of *Mississippi: An American Journey* and coeditor (with Michael S. Harper) of *The Vintage Book of African American Poetry*.

Ward, Geoffrey C. is a historian, screenwriter and a coauthor (with Ric Burns and Ken Burns) of *The Civil War: An Illustrated History*.

Ward, Jerry W., Jr. is the Lawrence Durgin Professor of Literature at Tougaloo College. He is the editor of *Trouble the Water: 250 Years of African-American Poetry* and coeditor (with John Oliver Killens) of *Black Southern Voices: An Anthology of Fiction, Poetry, Drama, Nonfiction, and Critical Essays.*

Warren, Gwendolin Sims has performed with the Metropolitan Opera and throughout Europe. She is minister of music at the Allen African Methodist Episcopal Church in Queens, New York, and the author of *Ev'ry Time I Feel the Spirit: 101 Best-Loved Psalms, Hymns, and Spiritual Songs of the African-American Church.*

Washington, Booker T. (1856–1915) was an educator and spokesman for African American people. His autobiography, *Up From Slavery*, was published in 1901.

Waterman, Christopher Alan is chair of the Department of World Arts and Cultures at the University of California in Los Angeles, as well as an anthropologist and musician who specializes in the study of music and popular culture in Africa and the Americas. He is the author of *Jùjú: A Social History and Ethnography of an African Popular Music*.

Wells, Ida B. (1862–1931) began speaking out against lynching as the editor of a small newspaper for blacks in Memphis, Tennessee. Her books include *The Memphis Diary of Ida B. Wells* and *Southern Horrors and Other Writings: The Anti-Lynching Campaign of Ida B. Wells, 1892–1900*.

Welsing, Frances Cress is a clinical psychiatrist in private practice in Washington, D.C., specializing in African American mental health. She is the founder of the Welsing Institute and author of *The Isis Papers: The Keys to the Colors* and *The Cress Theory of Color-Confrontation and Racism*.

Wesley, Valerie Wilson is a former executive editor of *Essence* magazine. She writes fiction and nonfiction for both adults and children. Ms. Wesley is most known for her Tamara Hayle mystery series, including *When Death Comes Stealing, Devil's Gonna Get Him, The Devil Riding* and *I'm Always True to You in My Fashion*.

West, Dorothy (1907–1998) was the last of the Harlem Renaissance writers. She was a short-story writer, editor and journalist, primarily for the *Vineyard Gazette*. Her first book, *The Living Is Easy*, was published in 1948. Her second work of fiction, *The Wedding*, was not published until 1995.

White, Graham is an Australian historian. He coauthored (with Shane White) *Stylin': African American Expressive Culture from Its Beginnings to the Zoot Suit*.

White, Shane is a professor in the History department at the University of Sydney. He wrote *Somewhat More Independent:*

The End of Slavery in New York City 1770–1810 and coauthored (with Graham White) *Stylin': African American Expressive Culture, from Its Beginnings to the Zoot Suit.*

White, Walter (1893–1955) was the secretary of the National Association for the Advancement of Colored People from 1918 until his death. He is the author of *Rope and Faggot: A Biography of Judge Lynch, The Fire in the Flint: A Young Doctor's Tragic Confrontation with the Segregated South* and *A Man Called White: The Autobiography of Walter White.*

Whitehead, Colson is a former television critic for *The Village Voice.* He is the author of *The Intuitionist* and *John Henry Days,* and a MacArthur Genius Award recipient.

Wideman, John Edgar is an author, scholar and educator. He is the first writer to win the PEN/Faulkner Award twice, in 1984 for *Sent for You Yesterday* and in 1990 for *Philadelphia Fire.* His other works include *The Homewood Trilogy, Brothers and Keepers* and *My Soul Has Grown Deep: Classics of Early African-American Literature* (editor).

Williams, Chancellor (1898–1992) was a historian, editor, high school teacher, principal and economist. His best-known works are *The Destruction of Black Civilization: Great Issues of a Race from 4500 B.C. to 2000 A.D.* and *The Rebirth of African Civilizations.*

Williams, Juan is a journalist and senior correspondent with National Public Radio. He is the author of PBS series companions *Eyes on the Prize: America's Civil Rights Years, 1954–1965* and *This Far by Faith: Stories from the African American Religious Experience.*

Williams, Sherley Ann (1949–2003) was the author of the 1992 Caldecott-winner *Working Cotton* and the slave narrative *Dessa Rose.*

Willis, Deborah is the curator of Smithsonian's Center for African American History and Culture. She is known for her photographic essays of the African American experiences such as her work in *Reflections in Black: A History of Black Photographers, 1840 to the Present.*

Wilson, Harriet E. (1828–1863) was the author of the novel *Our Nig; or, Sketches from the Life of a Free Black, in a Two-Story White House, North: Showing That Slavery's Shadows Fall Even There.* Very little is known about her life outside of what is written in her book.

Winchester, Faith is the author of the Read-and-Discover Ethnic Holidays series of cultural holidays including African American Holidays.

Wisniewski, David is an actor, special effects/prop designer and puppeteer, and a graduate of the Ringling Brothers and Barnum & Bailey Clown College. Wisniewskis's first children's book was *The Warrior and the Wise Man,* which was followed by *Elfwyn's Saga, Rain Player* and *Sundiata: The Lion King of Mali.*

Woodson, Carter G. (1875–1950) is known as the father of black history. He was a teacher, historian, publisher and the author of *The Mis-education of the Negro.*

Wright, Richard (1908–1960) was among the first African American writers to achieve literary fame and fortune. He is best known for his novel *Native Son* and his autobiography, *Black Boy.*

— X —

X, Malcolm (1925–1965) was one of the most influential African American leaders of the 1950s and 1960s. His autobiography is *The Autobiography of Malcolm X,* written with Alex Haley.

— Y —

Yarbrough, Camille is an actor, dancer, spoken-word artist and author. She is most known for her Coretta Scott King Award–winning book *Cornrows*.

Yetman, Norman R. is department chair of American Studies at the University of Kansas. He is the editor of *Majority and Minority: The Dynamics of Race and Ethnicity in American Life* and *Voices from Slavery: 100 Authentic Slave Narratives* and several other scholarly texts and publications.

About the Author

DOROTHY L. FEREBEE is a staff journalist on National Public Radio's *Fresh Air with Terry Gross* since 1990 and is the creator of the website BooksforBlacks.net. She has been a book reviewer for the National Newspaper Publishers Association's two hundred black newspapers, as well as the *Baltimore Sun*'s *Jubilee* magazine and Martha's Vineyard *North Star*.

She lives in Upper Darby, Pennsylvania.